BIBLE STORIES

BIBLE

·

STORIES

FROM THE OLD AND NEW TESTAMENT

Retold by
Leo Pavlát and Zuzana Holasová

Illustrated by Hedvika Vilgusová

CHARTWELL
BOOKS INC

Published by
CHARTWELL BOOKS, INC.
A Division of BOOK SALES. INC.
110 Enterprise Avenue
Secaucus, New Jersey 07094

This edition published 1993 by Sunburst Books,
Deacon House, 65 Old Church Street, London SW3 5BS.

Text by Leo Pavlát (The Old Testament)
and Zuzana Holasová (The New Testament)
Illustrations by Hedvika Vilgusová
Translated by Stephen Finn
Graphic design by Václav Konečný
© Aventinum, Prague 1991

ISBN 0 7858 0013 1

Printed in Slovakia by Neografia, Martin
1/23/06/51-01

Contents

Before you start to read...

Millions of books have been written all over the world throughout the course of time. There are those that people read and forget, and those they read over and over again. There are books that are popular in their day, and books which are passed on from generation to generation, a treasured legacy. One of the greatest of these is the Bible.

The name is derived from the Greek word 'b i b l o s' which means 'books', and the Bible is truly made up of many different books, all of them very old and full of wise teachings. They tell of God and of the world He created, of man, with whom God made a covenant, of human faith and defiance, and of deeds both good and evil.

The first part of the Bible, the older one, was written in Hebrew, and to this day forms the basis of Judaism, the religion of the Jews. The Jewish name for the Bible is the T a n a k h, formed in part from the initial letters of the three most important parts into which it is divided. They are called the Five Books of Moses (in Hebrew the T o r a h), the Book of Prophets (the N e v i i m) and the Writings (the K e t u - b i m). The T o r a h is of special importance to the Jews. In all, this first part of the Bible contains thirty-nine books.

The T a n a k h is usually called the Old Testament, because it is often put together with the Christian Gospels, or the New Testament. The New Testament contains twenty-seven books, and was originally written in Greek. It, too, had many authors. The most important of these were the Evangelists (Matthew, Mark, Luke and John), Apostles who wrote of the life, teachings, death and resurrection of Jesus Christ. The New Testament also includes the Acts of the Apostles and many Epistles, or letters, and the Book of Revelations.

Here you will find only a small selection of the many stories which appear in the pages of the Bible. The stories which have been chosen are already well known, and are rich in action and teaching. This book does not attempt to be a detailed account, rather, it is an introduction to a glimpse in to a unique work of literature, which has rightly earned the title Book of Books.

The Bible has already been translated into hundreds of languages, and its characters and stories have been reflected in countless examples of literature, painting, sculpture, music, and architecture. It is a book which has for two thousand years given inspiration to many different people, as a basis in forming their cultures. For human society, the Bible has never been an ordinary book. It has become something much more: for many people it bears witness to God's presence in our world. Millions of people have studied the Bible, looking upon it with awe, as their only book of faith, and an invitation to lead their lives by its teachings.

The Old Testament

The Creation

Before God created the world, there was nothing anywhere: no stars, planets, seas, clouds, animals, plants or people. Nothing. Everything was a dark, airless space which stretched on forever. The only Lord in this vast, never-ending emptiness was God, who had always been there and always will be. God is wonderful and can make anything happen. When, in the beginning, He created Heaven and Earth, He said, 'Let there be light!' and there was light. On one side lay pitch black darkness and on the other a shimmering light. 'The light shall be called day and the darkness night,' said God, and so the first day of creation was at an end.

On the second day God said, 'Let the vault of Heaven envelop the world.'

At that moment, above the empty, newly formed Earth there unfolded a heaven full of enormous clouds. The clouds slowly drifted from horizon to horizon, and down below on the Earth great waters flowed in chasmic depths.

God's work grew, and the second day of creation also came to an end.

On the third day God turned to the waters on the Earth. 'Come together in one place,' He told them.

With a mighty roar, huge waves flowed where God directed them and mighty streams cut channels through the Earth. From the waters emerged tall mountains, rolling hills and deep valleys.

'The dry Earth shall be called the land and the waters the sea,' God proclaimed, and was pleased with His work. Next, God introduced life to the world. The land turned green with grass and the leaves of trees and brilliant flowers lit up the meadows. The whole world was filled with the delicious fragrance of a thousand fruits. So the third day of creation passed.

On the fourth day God said, 'Let there be great lights in the sky to separate day from night. Let the larger light rule by day and the smaller by night.'

God had spoken and the Sun and the Moon appeared in the sky. When the Sun sank below the horizon, the Moon came out, and around it gathered thousands of distant, twinkling stars. The time of day replaced the time of night and the world grew even more beautiful. The fourth day of creation was complete.

The fifth day began. The Earth was resplendent with wonderful trees and flowers, but for all that it was not com-

plete. God had created a plant kingdom, but there were no living creatures on the Earth. Then God said, 'Let the waters teem with fish and sea creatures. Let birds take to the skies of the world.'

Hardly had the sound of God's voice died away, when the sea swarmed with the silvery bodies of fish. At the same time, beneath the canopy of Heaven, a beautiful song rang out as the birds thanked their Creator for the gift of life. God saw that He had done well and blessed the fish and the birds. So the fifth day of creation ended.

On the sixth day God commanded living creatures to appear on the dry land too.

Animals with hooves and claws, creatures which could run on all fours and others which dwelled in the crowns of the trees and beneath the ground filled the world. Then God said to Himself, 'The time has come to create a being that is more exalted than all the rest. I shall give him the gift of speech and free will and I shall also entrust to him the world that I have created.'

So God reflected and created man. He made him from the Earth, but into his body of dust He breathed an invisible soul. In this way, man was created in God's image and God was pleased with what He had done. The sixth day of creation was at an end.

The Creation

On the seventh day God's work was ended. How beautiful was this world He had created! Nothingness and emptiness had reigned before the beginning of creation. Now, the waters and the mountains, the darkness and the wind sang praise to God, the plants and living creatures bowed down to Him.

In six days God created the world, but on the seventh day He completed it. On this day He gave the world the greatest gift of all: the gift of rest.

Only now was God's work done. The whole of creation wondered at God's wisdom, rejoiced in the Creator's love and in the peace of the seventh day.

God blessed this day and made it holy. 'It shall be forever sacred to me,' He said, 'for this is the most precious day in the whole week. On this day let man rest and remember what I have done.'

So God had finished His work of creation, and the world abounded with His wisdom, mercy and love.

The Disobedience of Adam and Eve

The first man was called Adam. In God's language this word sounded like the Earth and no other name was thus more fitting for man. God made Adam from the soil and also gave him the gift of the most beautiful place in the whole world. It was called the Garden of Eden. God brought Adam to the garden, far away on the Earth's eastern side. In Eden there rose a large river. With its crystal clear water it gave life to the plants, which never withered. Nowhere were there such beautiful flowers as those that grew in Eden, nowhere was the grass so lush and soft, and nowhere were the trees so slender and strong.

God led Adam through the whole garden. He told him to take care of it, so it would always remain so beautiful, and Adam promised God that he would look after the garden. Finally God brought Adam to the very centre of Eden. Here two trees grew: the Tree of Eternal Life and the Tree of Knowledge of Good and Evil. God pointed to this tree and said, 'You may eat from all the trees in the garden, Adam, except from the Tree of Knowledge of Good and Evil. I created you so you would live forever. You live in a garden of peace and delight. On the day that you try to taste the fruit of the Tree of Knowledge you will lose the gift of eternal life and so one day will die.'

This time, too, Adam promised that he would do what God asked him. He had no need to worry about food. The garden had plenty of other trees with juicy fruits, and when Adam felt hungry he could eat his fill. He rested in the soft grass under the trees, refreshed himself in the water of the river and once more returned to the work God had given him. He was pleased to be part of God's work, and his reward was eternal life in the company of God.

There was only one thing which troubled Adam: he was alone in the world. The animals in the Garden of Eden lived in pairs; male and female together. They played and fell asleep beside each other, but Adam had no one to speak to. He did not have a companion who would understand him. He did not have anyone who would belong to him.

God knew of Adam's sadness and wanted to make him happy. He put Adam into a deep sleep, and while he slept He took one of Adam's ribs. God let flesh grow in its place, and from the rib He created a woman. Then he woke Adam and said to him, 'Look, I have made a partner for

you. She will make your life whole, and be your helper. Be happy and bring children into the world. Your wife will give them life. So she will be called Eve – the mother of all life.'

Adam was very happy. 'I am so pleased to have you,' he told Eve. 'You were made from my body and we will always belong to each other!' He took his wife by the hand and walked with her through the whole garden. He told her about the work that God had entrusted to him and showed her the animals and the plants. From then on he did not leave Eve's side for a moment. They worked together and rested together, and together they praised God's love and goodness.

In the Garden of Eden, however, there lived a strange creature called a serpent. No other creature was able to speak except the serpent, which spoke like a man. It was the cleverest of all the animals, but

The Disobedience of Adam and Eve

its mind was always busy thinking of ways to trap and trick the first people. More than anything it wanted to make them do something evil. It watched Adam and Eve day and night.

One day, Adam and Eve were working near the Tree of Knowledge of Good and Evil. Adam told Eve about the tree and its forbidden fruit, but this was the first time she had been close to it. She longed to go closer still, almost as though some invisible force were drawing her nearer. Quietly, so that Adam did not hear her, she crept through the bushes until she was standing beside it. At that very moment she noticed the serpent, coiled in its branches. The creature had a melancholy look on its face and this made Eve feel sad too.

'How unhappy you are,' it sighed. 'I have heard that neither you nor Adam are allowed to do as you wish. Why, I believe you cannot even eat what you want. Wouldn't you like to try this luscious fruit? Go on, try it.'

'We must not eat from one tree only, the Tree of Knowledge,' Eve said uncertainly. 'If we eat from it, we would die.'

'Why should you die?' the serpent tried to dissuade her. 'On the contrary you will be the wiser. On the day you will eat the

forbidden fruit your eyes will be opened. You will see what you have not seen before, you will be like God, and also become the masters of good and evil; that is just what God does not want to. He wants to reign supreme, alone! He does not like you and therefore he threatens you.'

Eve thought for a moment. The serpent spoke sweetly and smoothly and its words seemed convincing. Such strange, brilliant light shone from its eyes that beside it even the colours of Eden paled. The trees in the garden began to look dull and grey, and were no longer beautiful to Eve. She had eyes for only one tree: the Tree of Knowledge of Good and Evil. It beguiled and enticed her, and she could not resist its lure. She forgot about God, Adam and the whole Garden of Eden, and could think of nothing but the round, ripe, luscious fruit which hung on the branch before her. The thought of it made her dizzy. 'If I taste this fruit, I will be wiser,' she said to herself. She reached out and picked one of the fruits and took a bite. Turning, she saw Adam walking towards her.

'Here, try it,' she invited.

Adam took the fruit and without asking any questions, ate it. Straight away they could see what they had not seen before. They were no wiser, as Eve had thought they would be, nor were they any more powerful. When they looked at their bodies, however, Adam and his wife saw that they were naked. They looked at their skin and saw it was as bare and smooth as the serpent's body, and at that moment they realized that the serpent had tricked them. Everything around them suddenly changed. The trees became stooped and the grass withered, and Adam and Eve were filled with sorrow. They no longer felt pleasure and happiness; they became afraid.

Then they heard God speak. 'Where are you?' He called to Adam.

Adam cowered in the darkest corner of the garden, pressing himself close to the ground so as not to be seen. He put his hands over his ears, but he could not escape God's voice. 'Where are you?' called the Creator, and Adam had no choice but to answer.

'I am ashamed to show myself because I am naked,' he said.

'Naked?' cried God. How do you know you are naked? You have not eaten from the Tree of Knowledge of Good and Evil, have you? You know that I forbade that!'

'Eve ate from it and gave me a taste,' said Adam, as though it were excuse enough.

'The serpent made me eat it,' said Eve.

God was very sad. 'What have you done?' He cried. 'Did I not warn you?' He turned to the serpent and said, 'For what you have done you will always be cursed. You will slither on your belly; you will lie in the dust and dust shall be your food. Adam and Eve have besmirched their souls and are no longer fit to live in paradise. The woman will have to bear great worries and the man's work shall be no more than toil. His fields will grow thistles and thorns and he will earn his bread by the sweat of his brow. So his days will pass, each one the same as the last, and in the end he will die. I made man from dust and to dust he will return.'

After these words God led Adam and Eve out of the Garden of Eden, and so man lost his gift of immortality. God summoned His cherubim and angels with fiery swords and he placed them in the Garden of Eden, telling them to stand guard over the Tree of Eternal Life lest man should once more be temped to pick its fruit.

Cain and Abel

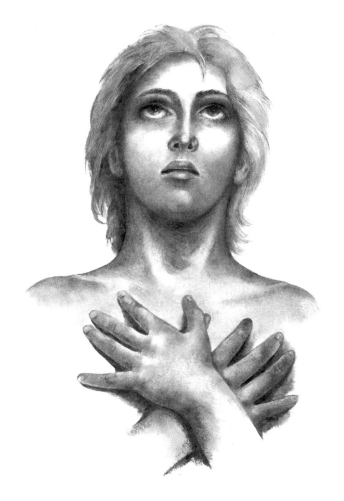

Adam and Eve settled to the east of the Garden of Eden on land that God had shown them. They took with them some tame animals, and these were their faithful companions. They learned to grow corn and bake bread from it, and as time passed, they gradually got used to their new life.

After some time Eve gave birth to a son. 'God has given me the gift of a son!' she cried happily and named her son according to these words. He was called Cain, which means *gift*. Later Eve gave birth to another son, Abel, or *breeze,* and the boys were like the names they bore.

God gave Cain many favours. When he grew up He gave him a large slot of land. He owned fields, meadows and orchards. God blessed his work and each year Cain enjoyed an abundant harvest. The more gifts God granted him, however, the more Cain wanted.

Cain's brother Abel was completely different. He did not rejoice in what he had, but in what he could give. He became a shepherd and looked after his flock with great love. He was as cheerful and gentle as a spring breeze and took his sheep to the places where the lushest grass grew.

While they were working, the two brothers often thought about God. 'If only He would give me more corn,' said Cain. 'Thank you, God, for giving me what you give me,' whispered Abel.

One day Cain and Abel decided to honour God for His gifts. 'We will burn a part

Cain and Abel

of our possessions on a fire as a sacrifice,'
they said. 'When the smoke reaches
Heaven, God will know that we have not
forgotten Him.'

Cain made the first sacrifice. Without
further thought, he took two ears of corn,
covered them with dry grass and set light
to them. As he gazed into the flames, his
thoughts were more about himself than

Cain and Abel

God. 'This sacrifice is good enough for God,' he thought. 'I was the one who sowed it and reaped it, not He.' Cain went away before the fire had even finished burning.

Then Abel made his sacrifice. First of all he brought some large, flat stones, and on them he laid the branches of fragrant trees. Then he looked at all his sheep carefully. He chose the strongest and most beautiful of them, the pride of his flock. 'It was God who gave life to sheep,' he said. 'They belong to Him, like everything else in the world.' He killed the sheep, laid it on the branches, and burnt its body. 'Thank you for looking after me, God,' he prayed. 'Thank you for your love.'

God saw the sacrifice of the two brothers, and heard their voices. He was pleased with what Abel had done, but seeing that Cain's gift was given only with the hope of gaining more He refused Cain's gift. So the smoke from Abel's fire climbed up into the clouds, coming close to Him; but the smoke from Cain's sacrifice blew away.

Cain saw that God had not accepted his gift, and he became very angry. How he

Cain and Abel

envied Abel! His face grew pale with rage.

Then God spoke to Cain. 'Why are you angry?' He asked. 'I know your thoughts, and I know they are not good ones. Be contrite, and I will accept your sacrifice. Be careful, in case you commit an evil deed. Sin is lying in wait for you like a wild beast stalking its prey, but if you wish, you can overcome it.'

God's voice fell silent. Cain looked around, and saw Abel, his brother, kneeling beside the sacrificial fire and bowing his head in obedience. Cain clenched his fist. 'I do not believe God's words,' he thought angrily. 'God does not really care about me, He loves Abel more. He refused to accept my sacrifice because of him!'

A terrible hatred rose in Cain's heart and he searched for a sharp stone. Walk-

ing up to Abel, he said, 'Come into the fields with me, brother.'

Abel stood up and followed Cain, and when they were in the fields, Cain threw himself upon Abel, who suspected nothing. He fell to the ground, and raising the stone high above his head Cain slew his brother.

Only then did Cain become calm again. Abel's head was bleeding and the blood soaked into the ground where it fell. Cain felt no pity for his brother. He turned and walked away.

Suddenly the voice of God thundered above Cain's head. 'Where is your brother Abel?' God demanded.

'I do not know,' Cain snapped back. 'Am I my brother's keeper?'

God was filled with wrath. 'What have you done?' He cried. 'Did I not warn you?

Cain and Abel

You have killed a man, you have spilled the blood which flows in your veins also. You are a murderer, and now the blood of the innocent calls out to me from the ground upon which it fell!'

Cain fell silent. He had not known God had seen the murder, but now he realized that God had seen everything. There was no excuse and Cain knew it. Cain hid his face, and God, whom no one can deceive, called out His judgement. 'The Earth shall be cursed where you have spilled blood. You shall leave this fertile land and wander the Earth as an outcast. No tree will hide you from the rain, nor will you find a helping hand. Torment shall be your master, and fear your companion.'

'How great is my guilt and sorrow,' Cain lamented. 'It is too great to live with. If no one will help me, someone might kill me. Take pity on me, God.'

Cain lifted his hands beseechingly, and God saw that he was truly sorry. God said to Cain, 'You will not be killed, Cain. You will stay alive, so that you may think about your crime. I will trouble you with regret, and your conscience will give you no sleep. That will be your punishment!'

At these words God put a sign on Cain's forehead to mark him out from the rest of mankind. Cain, weighed down with his guilt, set out on a long pilgrimage. He wandered through a desert land, and went further east, to the land of Nod, from where he never returned, and Adam and Eve never saw him again. So it was that the first people lost both of their sons on the same day. They were left alone, but God comforted them. After a time Eve gave birth to another son, Seth. Then she brought more sons and daughters into the world. The Earth filled with many people, but Abel's death and Cain's guilt were never forgotten.

Cain and Abel

The Flood

The first man, Adam, died, but his children and his children's children continued the work he had begun. They filled the land, looked after the animals and quickly learned new skills that made their lives easier. One of Adam and Eve's descendants, Jubal, had the idea that people could live in tents, and soon showed them how to make them. In this way, people could travel even to distant places carrying their shelter with them. In the evening they pitched camp and in the morning they would simply roll up their tents and set off on a new journey. They went with their herds further and further and entered new regions and lands. Another of Adam and Eve's descendants, Tubal-Cain, discovered how to smelt metal in the heat of the fire. From it he made strong, sharp metal tools and other people made knives and axes. They became skilled in their use and with the help of these tools their work became better. They quickly built large, spacious homes and in no time cities sprang up, and with them, market places. They were not unhappy. Jubal invented the flute and zither so that people could enjoy beautiful music. They did not live in harmony and peace for very long, however.

'Why should we toil in the fields?' they began to wonder. 'Let us wait until our neighbours' flocks grow and then we will take their sheep.'

'We can see that there are beautiful houses in the next city,' thought others, jealously. 'If we attack the city and kill the inhabitants, then their houses and possessions will belong to us!' Soon people began putting their thoughts into action.

Iron tools, which were supposed to serve mankind, were melted down and made into deadly weapons. People threw down their hoes and spades and took up spears and swords. Men killed each other without mercy.

Then God spoke. 'Man has destroyed the Earth I gave him. Blood is being spilled on all sides and brother has begun to fight brother in the search for wealth and power. The strong oppress the weak, and even the weakest look for someone to harm. I will destroy these people who care for no one except themselves. I will destroy them, and everything in which they find pleasure.'

At that time there was but one righteous man in the world. His name was Noah and he had three sons.

'Make an ark of cypress wood,' God told him, 'and line it with pitch. I shall

25

bring a great flood to the Earth, but you will be in the Ark and you will not die. Make a large, strong vessel and take on board with you your wife, all your sons and their wives. Take with you all the different animals, a male and a female of each species, so that no species will die out.'

Noah did what God had asked him. He felled some trees and began to build the Ark. It took many years to build, and it was not easy work.

'Noah, you are a fool,' the evil people laughed. 'Who ever saw a boat being built on dry land?'

'They say God told him to do it,' sneer-ed others. 'Noah is waiting for a flood! A flood that will never come!'

Noah did not answer them, and God saw that the people did not want to change their wicked ways. So it came that one day Noah had finished his task.

The Ark was three storeys high. It had one window and one door and Noah had carefully sealed all the little spaces between the boards with pitch so that water would not get in. Then he took inside enough food that the people and the animals would not go hungry.

When everything was ready, he began to let the first animals on to the Ark. Soon it rang with the cries of many different creatures. Lions and eagles, cows and dogs, ants, elephants, lizards and apes – all were there together. Pairs of every species found a place in the Ark and Noah showed them where they would live. Finally Noah himself boarded the Ark with his family. God sealed the door behind them and so began the Great Flood.

For seven days and seven nights the vessel stood on dry land as the sky grew darker, and the Sun disappeared. God spoke and it began to rain.

The heavens burst and torrents of water fell on the Earth. They pounded on the rocks, battered the fields and hammered on the roof of the Ark. The water came down as though the rivers of Heaven had burst their banks and the rivers of the Earth poured out on all sides, merging into lakes and great whirlpools, which sucked into their depths houses, trees, animals and people.

Only the Ark which Noah had built remained above the waves. The waters held it firmly in their grasp and the Ark floated even higher, even nearer the dark sky, from which the water continued to pour down. The rain continued day after day, week after week.

Then, after forty days and forty nights, God closed the founts of Heaven, and the rain stopped. The sinners had died in the torrents of water, but life had been preserved in the Ark. Noah's boat, with his family and the animals, rocked gently on the boundless surface of the water, and in the sky the Sun shone once more. The heat of its rays shrank the waters, until they began to draw back. It was to be another hundred and fifty days before the

Ark touched dry land, however. It came to rest on the top of Mount Ararat, and by this Noah knew that the waters of the Flood had begun to go down. He waited another forty days and then through the open window he released a raven.

'All living creatures are dead,' Noah said to himself, 'but the raven lives on dead bodies. If it finds food on dry land, it will surely not return.' But the raven flew hither and thither and each time it returned to Noah.

'I shall try releasing a dove,' thought Noah. 'Perhaps she will be the bearer of good news.' The dove left the Ark but returned just as exhausted as the raven had. The Earth was still covered in water and the dove had found no place to rest.

Noah waited another seven days and again released the dove. Towards evening the dove returned. In its beak it carried a freshly picked olive branch. Noah was very happy. 'Life is returning to the Earth!' he cried. 'Now it will soon be dry.' Once again he waited seven days and then he released the dove for the third time. This time the dove did not return. The Earth was dry and Noah heard God's voice. 'Leave the Ark,' He said, 'and take with you your wife, your sons and their wives. Release the animals into the fields and woods and let my Earth be bountiful once more.'

On hearing these words, Noah opened the doors of the Ark and the animals came out. The reptiles disappeared into the grass and under stones. The birds sang as they flew into the clouds and the other animals ran off in all directions. Only the tame creatures, which Noah had taken with him into the Ark in large numbers, remained close to people.

Noah felt grateful to be among the chosen few to survive the Flood. 'How good God is!' he thought. 'The world will be beautiful again!' He made a stone altar and made a sacrifice to the Creator.

God saw that Noah was making his sacrifice with a sincere heart. 'Noah,' He said, 'I brought the Flood to the world because people were killing and stealing. With this water I have destroyed all evil. I have cleansed the world so it will be without sin. Remember what I tell you now: Man must not murder. I shall make a contract with you and your descendants. I give you my word – the Flood will never again swallow the Earth. Spring will always follow winter and after summer there will be autumn. Night will give way to day and

day to night. The world will not vanish beneath the water and let the rainbow in the sky be an eternal reminder to man of my words.'

Noah looked up into the clouds. High above him he saw the rainbow. At one end it touched the Earth, then stretched up into the sky and down to the ground again. 'What a beautiful sign!' thought Noah. It was as if the rainbow was saying, 'Raise your eyes to God and He will look down on you from Heaven.'

The rainbow shone like a magnificent sparkling crown, its glittering arc forming a vault from horizon to horizon. A new life was beginning on Earth.

The Tower of Babel

Pious Noah had three sons, and after the Flood they became the forefathers of seventy different nations. Each nation was different, but they shared a common language. Even if children were born white, black or brown and if their eyes were slanted or round, they still understood each other as brothers. The nations were happy: they lived side by side and travelled the world in harmony.

One day people reached a valley in the land of Shinar. They had never seen such a beautiful place. The soil here was rich and fertile and there was just enough sun and rain. 'Even if we travel the whole world, we will never find a better spot,' they thought. 'Here we shall want for nothing.'

So they stayed in the land of Shinar and, indeed, they wanted for nothing. Their crops ripened more than once a year. The branches of the trees groaned under the weight of their fruit. Their sheep grew thick, heavy wool and gave sweet, creamy milk.

People soon became used to this abundance and began to think that their good fortune was due to their own hard work and quick thinking. At first some still thanked God for His gifts, but they, too, soon began to believe that the Earth was bountiful simply because they were good farmers. Pride entered people's hearts. The better things became, the less they thought of God.

'The world is in our hands,' they boasted when they reaped a rich harvest. 'We are its masters and no one else.'

'It is absolutely true,' agreed others. 'No one is equal to us.'

People became still more arrogant and self-important. In the land of Shinar, they learned to make bricks, and these replaced stones. First they shaped them from clay and then they baked them in the heat of the fire, saving much toil in the quarries.

'How marvellous we are!' they boasted. 'We can do whatever we want to! Let us go and build a wonderful city, greater than any which has ever been seen before. In it we will gather everyone together and we shall be even stronger and more powerful. No one shall divide us.'

'Let us build a tower,' other voices could be heard saying. 'Let its top reach the sky, so that everyone will know that we are the greatest and most powerful people. We will be celebrated throughout the world and no one will ever forget who we are!'

31

sands of bricks and setting in place huge piles of sand and lime and erecting tall wooden ladders. The building work continued with some speed, and soon the tower was several storeys high.

Then God looked down from Heaven. He saw the busy building work, heard the voices of the people and said to Himself, 'Man has forgotten me again. He imagines that his happiness is due to himself alone and does not want to know about me. He

There were others who cried, 'Our fame is greater than the glory of God Himself. We no longer need Him. We can live without Him.'

They set to work at once, making thou-

wonders at the work of his own hands, gives way to pride and hopes he will climb to Heaven on a stairway of bricks. How foolish people are! Once again they have embarked upon the road of evil. I shall destroy their work lest they commit an even greater sin.'

These were God's words and He caused people to speak in different tongues. They were no longer able to understand each other and immediately a great confusion began. All at once the workers building the city were unable to agree with each other.

'Give us bricks,' cried some, but instead of bricks their fellow builders gave them mortar.

'Give us mortar,' they cried a little later, and this time they were given bricks.

The work stopped suddenly and no one knew how to continue. The words of one person were just empty sounds to another. Squabbles and arguments broke out. On all sides cries and shouts could be heard. Finally the builders abandoned their work. Those who spoke one language gathered in one place. Those who spoke a different language settled a little further away.

As the nations no longer understood each other, neither did they trust each other, and were suspicious. Now people no longer wanted to live together. Boundaries were drawn and in their own land each nation spoke its own language.

It was not long before the valley in the land of Shinar became deserted. The nations scattered in all directions and all that was left of them was the half-built city and the tower. People called the place Babylon, which means babble. They thought they would achieve glory with their wonderful construction, but instead God revealed to them their own weakness. They wanted to live together to multiply their strength, but God, as a punishment, scattered them over the face of the Earth. In time the Tower of Babel collapsed, just as the people's dreams of their own great power had.

The Tower of Babel

The Calling of Abraham

each nation dreamed up their own idols and believed in their miraculous power.

At the time when people spread across the Earth, and each nation found its own new home, the name of God was once again forgotten. Each nation thought only of its own happiness. The people of one country glared at those of another and it did not occur to anyone that everyone was created by a single, all powerful, invisible God. Instead of Him,

Now there lived among the Chaldeans in the city of Ur-Kasdym a man whose name was Terah. His wife bore him three sons, Abram, Nahor and Haran. The people of Chaldea believed that the world was divided by fearsome gods. One god with a bull's head and sharp horns was supposed to rule the sky. They were very afraid of this god and another which had two lion's heads, which was supposed to

The Calling of Abraham

rule the underworld. They worshipped the gods of the Moon and the Sun, Storm, Fire and Water. They brought the best foods to their altar and hoped that by doing this they would be favoured by the gods.

The living God, however, is not the work of human hands. The God who created the world is its Lord. Of all the people He favoured Abram and told him, 'Leave this land where people worship abominable gods. Go away from this city in which people are corrupted by the servants of the stars. Live no more in your father's house. I will show you where you must go.'

Abram was already a fully grown man. He had no doubt about the power of God, so he took his wife Sarai and several servants, loaded all his belongings on to carts and set off.

It was not an easy journey. Before Abram had lived among people he knew well, but now he travelled to far off lands where people spoke in foreign tongues. He became a pilgrim without a home, a wanderer constantly threatened by danger. He trusted God's word, however, and God protected him. After a long journey He led Abram to a beautiful land. It was called Canaan.

'This land is for you and your children, and their children,' God told Abram. 'You were the only one who answered me when all had abandoned me, and so I am going to make you the father of a great nation. I will bless those who bless you, and curse those who do you wrong, for in your descendants all the nations of the Earth shall be blessed.'

After God had spoken, Abram built an altar to the Lord. He prayed to his Creator and God saw that Abram truly loved Him. He led Abram on his journey through Canaan and showed him its pastures, its mountains and streams. After travelling a long way, Abram stopped.

God spoke to him again. 'Abram,' He said, 'look around you. Look to the right, to the left, in front of you and behind you.

Your descendants will be as numerous as the dust on the ground. Should anyone manage to count the grains of dust, so shall be the number of your people's children.'

Although Abram was very happy, he and Sarai were no longer young and they still did not have a son. A year passed, and then another. The years were passing and still Abram's tent did not echo with the laughter of children.

On the plain of Mamre, not far from the place where Abram had settled, some trading routes crossed. The traders travelled from sea to sea, crossing huge deserts and with their goods they brought the smells of distant lands. Abram often gazed at the tracks the travellers left in the dust, and each time he did this he was reminded of God's words.

'My descendants will be like these grains of sand,' he pondered. 'After all this time we are still childless. I know God keeps His word. I shall wait.'

God knew what Abram was thinking, and when night fell, He spoke to him again. 'Come out,' said God, 'and look up.'

Abram obeyed. He looked up into the sky, where thousands of stars twinkled, and God said, 'Count the stars if you can. Your descendants will be as numerous.'

Abram believed God, but his wife Sarai was still unhappy. It bothered her that she had not given her husband a son, and one day, in a worried voice, she said to him, 'We have lived ten years in the Land of Canaan, and God has still not given me a son. Listen to what I say. Take my ser-

vant Hagar as your second wife. She will bear you the son that I have not brought into this world and your line will be preserved.'

Abram listened in amazement. He wanted nothing more than to fulfil God's promise at last, but he wanted the mother of his child to be Sarai, not her servant. Sarai went on begging Abram until he finally gave in, however, and he took the servant girl Hagar for his wife. Before the year was out Hagar had given birth to a son who was given the name Ishmael.

Before he saw the light of day, God said of the child, 'He will be wild. He will oppose everyone.'

'God knows everything,' thought Abram, 'but will Ishmael be a warrior if God's word is fulfilled? How could people bless the descendants of a warrior, men as violent as their father?'

Ishmael grew and Abram's worries grew too. Hagar was born in Egypt, a large land in which people no longer knew the true God and worshipped idols like the Chaldeans in Abram's native Babylonia.

'What if Hagar is telling the boy about Egyptian deities?' Abram worried. 'Will not Ishmael bow to wooden idols? Will not forget the one true God?'

How greatly God was trying His servant Abram! He gave him a son – and yet Abram could not rejoice. He endowed him with issue – and yet Abram could not believe he would be his chosen heir. Abram continued praying to God. His mouth was full of gratitude and God loved him for it. When Ishmael was thirteen, God appeared to Abram once more and said, 'Abram, I shall change your name. You will no longer be called Abram, the Noble Father, but Abraham, the Father of the Great Multitude. Your wife will no longer be called Sarai, the Princess, but Sarah, the Mother of Nations, and you will both be the forebears of kings.'

Abraham and Sarah were already both very old. Abraham wondered how such old people could have children.

God spoke again. 'Is anything impossible for me? I rule over everything. I give life and assign death. A son will be born to you and you will call him Isaac. I have chosen this, as I have chosen you.'

Abraham fell with his face to the ground. Such a long journey he had taken, and so often he had been filled with doubts, but his faith was strong. He spread God's truth throughout the world and God rewarded him: He gave to him and Sarah a new name. It was as though they had been reborn. God gave them the meaning of a new life. The vow to Abraham began to be fulfilled.

The Calling of Abraham

The Punishment of Sodom and Gomorrah

One day Abraham was sitting at the entrance to his tent. It was a very hot day. Abraham looked up. Next to his tent stood three men. Abraham was surprised, for he had not seen anyone approaching. He went to meet them and bowed low to the ground.

'Sir,' he addressed the first man, 'if I have found favour in your eyes, then please do not leave. I will bring you water to refresh your tired feet. I will bring you bread and you may rest in the shade of the trees.'

'Do as you have said,' agreed the men.

Abraham at once went off to see Sarah and asked her to mix some dough and bake some bread. He chose a calf from his herd, and left it to be killed and cooked for his guests. He offered them milk and butter and then sat a little distance away from them and watched them eat.

When they had refreshed themselves, they said, 'Abraham, we are not ordinary travellers, but the angels of the Lord. You did not recognize us, but you accepted us as your dearest guests. Now we know that you are not only faithful to God, but you are also a friend to your fellow man, and

for this you shall be rewarded. In a year from now Sarah shall give birth to the son that God foretold for you. He shall be your heir and the blessing of your race.' After these words God's messengers left and set off to the distant cities of Sodom and Gomorrah. They had come to Abraham as the bearers of glad tidings, but they went to Sodom and Gomorrah to pronounce God's judgement. For God had said, 'I hear a great clamour from Sodom and Gomorrah. The streets are full of violent men and lies rule instead of truth. So I shall destroy Sodom and Gomorrah and rid them of sin.'

Abraham was accompanying God's messengers, and he heard the Lord's voice. His heart was troubled.

'Lord,' he said humbly, 'perhaps there are also righteous people in Sodom. If there are fifty of them, will you destroy them along with those who perpetrate evil?'

'If I find fifty righteous people in Sodom, then I will forgive the godless ones too,' replied the Lord.

'What if there are five fewer righteous people than fifty?' Abraham went on. 'Will you destroy the whole city because of them?'

'If this is so,' said God, 'the city shall be spared.'

'Permit me to continue,' said Abraham to the Lord. 'What if there are only forty righteous people in Sodom?'

'I shall be content with that too,' replied God. 'If there are forty righteous people in Sodom, then I shall let the whole city survive.'

'What if there are only thirty?' whispered Abraham.

'Even thirty will be enough.'

'And what if there are no more than twenty?'

'Then I shall not destroy the city.'

'Please do not be angry, Lord, if I presume to speak once more,' Abraham asked the Lord. 'Perhaps there will only be ten righteous people in Sodom.'

'Then I shall also be merciful,' said God. 'If there are ten righteous people in Sodom, I shall not kill even those who have sinned.'

When Abraham had received this assurance, he said farewell to the messengers and returned home.

In the evening the messengers arrived in Sodom. The first person they saw was Lot, the son of Abraham's brother Haran. Lot was not as God-fearing as Abraham, but kept an open house. He bowed deeply to the men and said to them, 'Will you come to my house and spend the night here, and in the morning you can continue your travels.'

The men accepted Lot's hospitality. They ate the unleavened bread that he offered them and they were just going to sleep, when on the other side of the door they heard shouting. The men of Sodom had gathered on the street. Young and old alike were there and they surrounded the house on all sides, abusing Lot and threatening him. 'Where are the men who came

to your house?' they shouted. 'Give them to us now. We know what sort of welcome to give them.'

Lot went outside. 'Brothers,' he said to the inhabitants of Sodom, 'do not do anything evil, I beg you. Do not harm my guests. I would prefer my nearest and dearest to suffer, but please do not harm strangers to whom I offered shelter.'

'Are you going to be our judge?' shouted the mob. 'You yourself are a foreigner. We will treat you even worse than them.'

The men of Sodom attacked Lot. They had grabbed him and were just trying to break into the house, when God's messengers came to Lot's aid. They quickly pulled him inside and closed the door. They blinded all the men of Sodom so that they could not find the way in.

'Lot,' they said then, 'take all your relatives and lead them out of this city before we destroy it. The sin of Sodom and Gomorrah is too great. God sent us to destroy these cities, so do not delay.'

Lot did not want to leave Sodom. 'How could it be possible for the whole city to

The Punishment of Sodom and Gomorrah

be destroyed at once,' he said. He wanted to stay.

God's messengers urged Lot, however, 'Do not linger. Your life is in danger. Take your wife and your daughters and go, so that you do not die for the sins of others.'

The men left the house with Lot and took him and his family out of the city. Then they said, 'Run away and do not stop for a second until you have left this city of death and despair. Keep walking straight ahead and do not look back. God will punish this region. He will destroy Sodom and Gomorrah, but you will live.'

It was morning. The Sun was just rising when Lot, his wife and their two daughters left the land that God had promised to destroy. At that moment the Lord sent fire and brimstone down on Sodom and Gomorrah. Huge flames flared out of the sky. The earth began to sink and the houses collapsed. Sodom and Gomorrah were transformed into a raging furnace. In an instant people and animals perished and the fire destroyed the fields, the trees and the grass.

Lot fled. By his side were his two daughters, but his wife would not hurry. She heard the terrible noise, and unable to resist, turned around to witness God's judgement. She looked towards the fire and in an instant all life left her body. Lot's wife had been turned into a pillar of salt, an eternal reminder to those who do not listen to the word of God.

At that time Abraham was far from the place of destruction. When he looked in the direction of Sodom and Gomorrah, all he could see was smoke rising from the Earth. His appeal for life had been in vain. In Sodom and Gomorrah there were not even ten righteous men. Now thick smoke enveloped the cities. The wind scattered it in all directions until it completely disappeared.

Finally there was no longer a trace of any smoke, just as there was no trace of Sodom and Gomorrah.

The Punishment of Sodom and Gomorrah

The Trials
of Abraham

After a long time Abraham's wife Sarah finally gave birth to a son. Abraham named him according to God's instructions. He called him Isaac, which means *smiling person,* and indeed he brought only laughter and joy to Abraham and Sarah.

On the day when Sarah stopped suckling the boy, Abraham prepared a great feast. It began happily but ended sadly.

Ishmael, the elder son of Abraham and the Egyptian woman, Hagar, did not take any food or drink, but just taunted little Isaac. The taunts did not bother the child because he was too small to understand them, but Sarah was hurt by the cruel words.

'Why do I have to endure this mocking,' cried Sarah bitterly. 'Ishmael shall not abuse me!' She went to Abraham and said, 'Banish Ishmael and his mother Hagar. Throw them out so that I no longer have to see their sneering faces.'

Abraham was very sad. He loved Isaac as his chosen heir, but Ishmael was his son too. Could he throw him and Hagar out into the inhospitable wilderness? Could he harm his son so?

Abraham was plagued by doubts. Sarah's words tormented his heart. When he was suffering most, he heard God's voice saying, 'Do not torment yourself. Do as Sarah asks you. I will be with Ishmael and Hagar and I will protect them from all evil.'

45

'Let thy will be done,' said Abraham. Early in the morning he got up and gave Hagar bread and a water-skin. 'Take Ishmael and go,' he told her, but did not tell Hagar what God had said.

With a sad heart Hagar set out. As far as the eye could see there was nothing but endless wilderness. Her feet sank into the sand. The Sun burnt down and there was no shade to be found. After a time Hagar stopped. She had some food and drank from their water-skin and Ishmael ate and drank too. So they travelled on together until there was not even a drop of water left in the water-skin.

Hagar sank to her knees. 'What am I going to do?' she wailed. 'Where shall I find water in the middle of the desert?'

She looked at her son and was filled with anguish. She fell to the ground in sorrow. 'I do not want to see Ishmael die of thirst,' she cried. She sat down a little way away and wept bitterly.

Suddenly she heard God's voice. 'Do not despair, Hagar. I will not let the boy die. He shall live.'

At that moment Hagar saw something that she had not noticed earlier. Right in front of her was a well, filled to the brim with clear spring water. Hagar quickly plunged the water-skin into it. She gave Ishmael water to drink and refreshed herself too. The danger had passed. She and her son were saved.

Several years passed. Hagar settled in the distant plain of Paran and her son Ishmael grew into a sturdy and strong man. Far away from there, in Abraham's house, Ishmael's brother Isaac was growing, too. Abraham taught him to fear God, and to be strong and good. He did what his Creator had asked him and God said to himself, 'There is no one in the whole world like Abraham. When I told him to leave his birthplace, he obeyed without question and left his home, his relations and his friends. I assured him that in his old age I would give him a child. I want people to remember Abraham always and to learn from his strong faith. Everything I want is good for people, even when it sometimes seems difficult to them. This is why I am subjecting Abraham to the last trial.

I know that he will hold out and will become even better than before.'

So God thought and said, 'Abraham, take Isaac, the son of all your hopes, and go with him to the land of Mori. Take him to the mountain I shall show you, and sacrifice him to me.'

Abraham hung his head. What a terrible thing God wanted him to do; but Abraham believed in God, so he did as his Maker had told him. Early the next morning he got up. He woke Isaac and two servants, chopped wood for the sacrificial fire, and saddled a donkey. He loaded the wood on the animal's back, and the four of them set out.

Abraham was sad. If he had been asked to give away all he possessed, he would not have left himself a single sandal. He would have done anything to fulfil God's will. Sacrificing his son was a different matter, however. He had spent so many years looking forward to the birth of his child. How could God take him away now?

So the day came to an end. Abraham was sad and confused. 'If I kill Isaac,' he thought, 'I shall never have any descendants; but God never fails to keep his word. Did he not once say that his nation would be as numerous as the stars in Heaven?'

At last, on the third day, he could see the place of sacrifice in the distance. He ordered the servants to wait for him, and he and his son carried on. Isaac carried the firewood on his back, and Abraham held

The Trials of Abraham

a knife in his hands. Silently, they went up the side of the mountain, and when they reached its top they stopped. Abraham built an altar, arranged the firewood on top of it, tied Isaac carefully and laid him on the firewood. Picking up the knife, he raised his arm.

At that moment a voice rang out from Heaven. 'Abraham,' God's angel called, 'do not harm Isaac. The Creator was testing you, and you have passed the test. You have proven beyond anything that you would do God's will, and hold Him dearer than anything on Earth. Therefore, may you be blessed.'

Abraham quickly untied Isaac and held him close. He could feel his heart beating, and his warm breath on his face. 'My son will live,' he rejoiced. 'Isaac is alive!'

They stood embraced for some time, and Abraham's happiness knew no bounds. Suddenly, he raised his eyes and saw a goat whose horns had become tangled in the bushes. 'God Himself has sent me a sacrificial goat,' Abraham thought. He set the creature free and sacrificed it on the altar instead of his son. As he did so he prayed, and he had never been closer to God than at that moment. The Creator had led him along a path which was a far from easy one, but Abraham had listened to the voice of God, and God had given him the strength to overcome all obstacles.

The sacrificial fire slowly died down. Abraham and his son travelled back down the mountain to where the servants were waiting, and they went home together. It was a much easier journey this time.

The Trials of Abraham

A Bride for Isaac

Abraham had passed all the tests, and had God's blessing. God granted him large herds of cattle and sheep, along with camels and donkeys. He was given many servants, and great wealth. Eventually, however, Sarah died, and apart from grief, this gave Abraham reason to worry. He was an old man, and his life was behind him, but his son Isaac was a young man and had not taken a wife.

'I might die one day,' thought Abraham, 'and then Isaac will be left alone. I have taught him to have faith in God, and his wife must do the same. In this land the people worship idols and images, not the true God. How is Isaac to find a wife from among them?'

Abraham called his servant Eliezer, whom he had once brought from the faraway city of Damascus, and said to him, 'You have been living here for many years, and have served me faithfully all that time. I trust you. You are the only one who can help me.'

'I will do as you ask,' replied Eliezer. 'What do you want me to do?'

'Go to my native Babylonia,' Abraham told him. 'Visit the place where God once spoke to me, and bring from there a suitable wife for my son Isaac.'

'What if I find such a woman and she will not return with me?' asked Eliezer. 'Am I to take your son back to Babylonia with me?'

'No, that you must not do!' cried Abraham. 'This land of Canaan was promised me by God. He set it aside for my descendants, and Isaac must marry here. Go on your way, for God will send His angel before you, and you will return with a bride chosen by the Lord Himself. Isaac will marry her, and when I, too, am dead, he and his wife will carry on the work Sarah and I have begun.'

Eliezer swore he would do everything Abraham asked him to, and set out on his journey. He took with him a number of guides, ten camels, and precious gifts, and after many days' journey reached the city of Aram-naharijim in Babylonia. It was late in the afternoon when Eliezer stopped beside a well to water the tired beasts, and it was only then that he realized how difficult his task was going to be. At that time of day there were many young girls going to the well to draw water, but how was Eliezer to know which was the right one?

Eliezer began to pray. 'God of my mas-

ter Abraham,' he whispered, 'show me mercy, I pray; grant success to my work.'

Eliezer became lost in prayer, and he suddenly thought, 'No one is as kind as Abraham. He helps all travellers, and likes to look after strangers. I will ask the next girl who comes here for a little water. If she gives me a drink from her jug, and does not allow my animals to go thirsty either, she will be as kind as he. Only such a girl is worthy to be Isaac's wife.'

No sooner had Eliezer decided what to do, than a beautiful young maiden came up to the well with a jug on her shoulder.

Eliezer had never seen such beauty, but he was more concerned that the girl should have a kind heart than a pretty face. He waited for her to fill her jug, then he said to her, 'Give me a drink of water from your jug.'

'Help yourself, sir,' said the girl with a smile. She quickly pulled up the jug and gave it to Eliezer.

When Eliezer had refreshed himself, the girl said, 'Rest while I water your animals.' She did not even wait for Eliezer's reply and poured the rest of the water into a trough for the camels and hurried back

to the well. She came back with a full jug, emptied it again and went back and forth several times until all the animals had been watered.

Eliezer watched the girl in amazement. 'This beautiful girl has never seen me before, but without hesitation she showed compassion towards me and my animals,' he thought.

In thanks, the servant gave the girl one golden earring and two golden bracelets and asked the name of her father.

'I am Rebecca, the daughter of Bethuel,' she replied.

Eliezer asked her some more questions and found that she was from the same tribe as Abraham. Abraham's servant was very happy. 'May I sleep in your father's house?' he asked the girl.

'Of course,' she replied. 'We have plenty of room and also straw and food for your camels.'

Now Eliezer had no doubts about the girl's goodness. He fell to his knees and thanked God for His help. The girl ran home and told her parents and brothers what had happened to her and showed them the golden earring and the two beautiful golden bracelets that Eliezer had given her.

Rebecca had a brother named Laban. He had no time for poor travellers, but was happy to welcome rich pilgrims. When he saw the gifts that Eliezer had given his sister, he ran to meet him. 'It is not an opportunity to be missed,' he thought to himself. 'I must make him welcome.' He unharnessed Eliezer's camels, gave them plenty of food to eat, and led Eliezer and his guide into the house of his father, Bethuel. He sat at the fully-laden table and in his heart he hoped that he, too, would gain something from this unexpected visit.

Eliezer was hungry after his long journey, but he did not forget for one moment why he had travelled so far. 'I will not eat,' he said, 'until I have told you why I have come.'

'Speak on,' said Laban.

Abraham's servant then spoke about the oath he had sworn to his master. He told Laban he had come to find a bride for Isaac and recounted his prayer by the well and Rebecca's kindness.

'She did exactly what I asked of her,' said Eliezer, finishing his story. 'God wanted it to be this way and I know that if I were to look for ever I would never find a more beautiful bride for Isaac than your sister. Please show mercy to my master and allow Rebecca to become Isaac's wife.'

Laban and his father Bethuel listened to their guest carefully. They did not know about God and had no fear of Him. How-

ever, when they heard about the miracle at the well, they said together, 'God has decided and we cannot change a thing. Take Rebecca with you to the Land of Canaan so she can become your master's wife.'

At these words, Eliezer fell to the ground and praised the Lord. He told his servant to bring gifts of gold and silver and cloth from foreign lands. Again he gave presents to Rebecca and to Laban and the bride's mother. The marriage contract was concluded. They all began to eat and they feasted and made merry long into the night.

The next day, however, Laban and his mother were sorry that they had agreed so quickly. 'We were foolish,' they said to each other. 'We should have let these rich

A Bride for Isaac

guests stay longer. The longer they are with us, the more gifts we shall receive.' Neither Laban nor his mother wanted to break their word, however, and so they tried to get round Eliezer. When he was about to leave the next morning with his guides, they said, 'We love Rebecca very much. It will be hard for us without her. Let her stay just a little longer. Ten days will be enough and then she can leave.'

'Do not detain me,' Eliezer replied. 'God has blessed my journey, so let me go as we agreed.'

Laban and his mother saw that persuasion would not work, so they resorted to cunning. 'We have given you Rebecca,' they said to Eliezer, 'but we do not know if she wants to marry. Let Rebecca say what she wants.'

Straight away they summoned the girl and asked her, 'Are you going with this man?'

Laban and his mother were sure that Rebecca would refuse. 'Why would she want to go to a foreign land,' they thought. 'Does she lack anything here at home? She was born in Babylonia and she has her family and friends here. Why would she give herself to a husband she does not even know?'

Much to their surprise, Rebecca did not hesitate for a moment. The God that Eliezer had spoken about had become her God too. She believed in His power, and so she said firmly, 'I am going.'

Neither Laban nor his mother could stop the girl. They sent with Rebecca her favourite servant, and Bethuel blessed her as Eliezer's caravan set off once more.

Isaac was in the field, thinking, that evening when on the horizon he saw a long line of camels.

Seeing Isaac in the distance, Rebecca asked, 'Who is that man?'

'My master, your husband,' replied Eliezer.

On hearing these words, Rebecca sat on the ground. She covered her face, as was the ancient custom, and the veil hid her beauty until after the wedding. Isaac took Rebecca to the tent of his mother Sarah, and so Abraham's wish was granted: his son had got a bride as pure and good as his own.

A Bride for Isaac

Isaac's Blessing

Isaac was as dear to God as his father Abraham. The Creator loved Isaac but his wife Rebecca did not have children. 'God,' prayed Isaac. 'Grant me an heir, so that my tribe shall flourish and spread the glory of your name.'

God always hears the prayers of the good, and so Rebecca soon became pregnant with twins. They pushed and shoved so much inside her that she asked God if He could tell her why they behaved in this strange way.

'Do not be afraid,' said God. 'I shall tell you what will happen. You will give birth to two sons and they will be the fathers of two nations. One will bear a grudge against the other and they will go their separate ways. The first son will be stronger than the second but the older will be the servant of the younger.'

'God has revealed to me which son He has chosen,' thought Rebecca. 'He has let me into His secret and I shall do everything to see that God's will is fulfilled.'

She did not tell anyone about the Lord's words, however. She locked them in her heart and waited patiently to see what the future would bring.

At the appointed time Rebecca gave birth to two sons. The first was covered from head to toe in thick red hair. They gave him the name Esau. Then the second son appeared, holding Esau by the heel, as if they were fighting. This son got the name Jacob. One son would bear a grudge against the other, the older would be the servant of the younger. Rebecca remembered God' prophecy. God had chosen Jacob. And so, although she loved both sons, Jacob was closer to her.

Esau and Jacob grew up, and Rebecca could see that they were exactly as God had foretold. Esau became brave and fearless, a strong fellow whom none dared challenge. He spent days on end in the fields and forests with his knife in his hand, leading the wild life of a hunter. Jacob was just the opposite of his brother. He couldn't bring himself to kill any animal, but remained quiet and peaceful. He was as pure as the day he was born and wished nothing more than to serve God as faithfully as had his grandfather Abraham and his father Isaac.

Esau and Jacob loved their father equally well, but Esau was the one who won his heart. Every time he went hunting he brought Isaac some game, and he heaped gifts upon him. Isaac therefore thought that Esau loved him more dearly than his brother, and he showed him favour. Rebecca was often sad over this; she spent more time with her sons than their father did, and she knew what they were like inside. She saw what a ruthless and cruel hunter Esau was, and how skilfully he set traps and snares. 'Isaac had been trapped by him,' she thought. 'He pretends to be faithful to him so as to win his favour, but he does not deserve Isaac's trust.'

It was not long before Esau proved Rebecca right.

One day he came home tired and hungry. As he looked around for something to eat, he saw Jacob cooking some lentils.

'Give me your food,' he told his brother, 'I have been out hunting all day and I should like to eat.'

Jacob looked at his brother. Esau's clothes were spattered with the blood of animals and his eyes burned with a wild fire. 'Why was I not the first-born?' he thought. 'Why should Esau be my father's heir, just because he is older? Doesn't my father love the Lord? Esau is not fit to take

my father's place. He does not give his life for God, or bow to His will.'

Then Jacob had an idea: he would buy his brother's birthright from him. Esau did not place great store by it anyway; but Jacob knew what a privilege it was – the privilege of the heir. So he pushed the food in front of Esau and said, 'Swear that you will sell me your birthright for this food.'

'Why not?' grinned Esau. 'I cannot eat my birthright; what use is it to me? I swear, for I do not consider it important.'

So it was that Esau sold his birthright. He ate and drank his fill, thinking more of his full stomach than of how he looked in the eyes of God. After some time he chose a bride from among the pagan Hittites. They worshipped false gods and mocked the one God, but Esau did not mind. He turned his face from the Creator and did not try to draw near Him.

Years went by, and Isaac grew old. His body became weak, and he could feel death approaching. Once God had blessed him in the same way as He had once blessed his father, Abraham. He gave them the strength to undergo a difficult journey, and promised success for whatever they did. Isaac wanted God to look after his heirs. He was thinking of Esau, not Jacob, although he was sad that Esau had married a pagan. 'With God's help I will bless Esau,' he thought, 'and he will serve the Creator like his forefathers. I will bind him with my words to do good deeds.' Rebecca knew God had decided otherwise.

By that time Isaac had gone quite blind. He called Esau to him and said, 'Go out into the fields and kill me some game. Cook a food which I enjoy, and I will bless you.'

Rebecca heard all this. The moment Esau had left with his bow and his quiver of arrows, she told Jacob, 'Choose a pair of fine goat kids from the herd. I will cook a dish your father likes. Bring them to me, and he will bless you instead of Esau.'

Jacob said, 'My brother is hairy, but I am not. If my father touches me, he will know I have tricked him.'

Rebecca was sure of herself however. Had not God revealed His will to her before the boys were born? So she said to him, 'Just do as I tell you. Whatever happens, I will take the blame.'

When he heard this, Jacob had no more objections. He brought the kids, and his mother made a tasty meal out of them. Then she took Esau's best clothes and dressed Jacob in them, winding the goat-skins round his arms and neck. Jacob went in to his father, and said, 'I have brought the dish you asked for.'

'How strange,' said Isaac. 'I could swear that was Jacob's voice. Come nearer, so that I can touch you.'

Jacob went up to his father, but Isaac was taken in because the arms he felt were just as hairy as Esau's. Then he ate the food in peace. After he had drunk a little wine, he said to Jacob, 'Kiss me.'

His son bent over him, and Isaac could smell Esau's clothes. He no longer doubted that it was really Esau. Then he placed his hands on Jacob's head and blessed him, 'Let God give you plenty of rain and good harvests. Let neither grain nor grapes be lacking. The nations will honour you, and you will be master over your brother. He who curses you, will be cursed himself, and he who blesses you will be blessed.'

The Lord Himself placed these words on Isaac's lips. He raised Jacob up above Esau, as Rebecca had foretold many years before, but the younger son did not know about this. He was afraid he would be found out, and quickly went away.

In a while Esau came in from the fields.

He, too, had prepared a tasty dish for his father. 'Get up,' he said to him, none too politely, 'and eat some of the game I have brought you.'

'Who are you?' Isaac asked, filled with confusion.

'Esau, your eldest son.'

Isaac was astounded. He realized that he had given his blessing to Jacob. Reaching his arms out to Esau, he said, 'I cannot bless you. Your brother came first.'

'What do you mean?' cried Esau. 'Was he not satisfied to take away my birthright? Did he have to steal my blessing too?'

How quickly Esau forgot what he had once promised to Jacob. He had sold him his birthright; it was he who had given up his right to be his father's heir. Now he realized the foolishness of his actions and wept, crying out, 'Bless me too, Father! Please, you must do something!'

Isaac was not a man to go back on his word however, and he said to Esau, 'I have blessed your brother, and I cannot change what I have said. I have made Jacob your master; it is he who will enjoy the riches of this land. You will live by the sword.'

Esau left angrily, and Jacob felt sorry for him; but he believed in the Lord, and the Lord soon showed him how wisely He rules the fate of men.

Esau was filled with rage. 'I will kill Jacob,' he said in hatred. 'I will take his life, and my father will be sorry.'

Rebecca and Isaac heard of his words and it caused them pain. It was only now

that Isaac saw his elder son's true nature. There was no time to lose. Rebecca ran to Jacob and told him, 'Your brother wants to kill you, so do as I tell you. He is stronger than you, and you must flee. When his anger passes, I will send for you.'

Jacob quickly made ready to leave. He said goodbye to his mother and then went to see his father, Isaac. Isaac embraced his son. Then Jacob knelt in front of him and Isaac blessed him one more time. 'May the almighty God grant you many descendants,' he said. 'May He go with you as He went with Abraham, so that you may live in peace in the land He gave him.'

This time Rebecca did not need to deceive Isaac. He blessed Jacob willingly, sure that he was the only one who could carry on the work God had set aside for his race.

Isaac's Blessing

*Jacob's
Tribulation*

J acob fled from Esau. On his way he
met rich merchants driving waggons
filled with precious goods, but all he had
was a staff on which to lean. He passed pilgrims who shared the enjoyment of their
long journey, but no one went with him.
He was quite alone.

Before he left his father's house, Rebecca had said to him, 'Go to Laban, my
brother, who lives in Haran. You will be
safe there.'

So Jacob went eastwards, into the land
of Mesopotamia. He hurried, so as to escape his brother's wrath, and his heart was
heavy. Towards evening he reached a solitary spot. The Sun was setting, and Jacob
lay down on the bare ground to rest. He
laid his head on a stone and closed his
eyes. The moment he fell asleep, he had
a dream. He saw a ladder reaching up to
the sky, along which the angels of God
were climbing up and down. At the top of

the ladder stood God Himself, and Jacob heard him speak, 'Listen, Jacob; I am the God of your ancestors, Abraham and Isaac. Wherever you go I will protect you. The earth on which you are lying shall belong to your descendants, and I will never leave you.'

Jacob woke up. It was broad daylight. In his mind's eye he could still see the ladder with its heavenly messengers, and his soul was filled with joy. God had spoken to him; He had shown him the ladder which joined together Heaven and Earth. No, Jacob was no longer unhappy. 'That God would give me the strength to serve Him faithfully,' he wished. 'May I return in peace to the house of my father.'

He took the stone he had laid his head upon, and raised it up in memory of the dream. 'This is the gate of Heaven,' he said, and he renamed the place *Bét-el* – House of God.

After a long journey, Jacob reached his mother's brother Laban's house in Haran. Laban was not a good man. Abraham's servant Eliezer had discovered that many years before, and Laban had not changed. He thought only of his own good, and was cunning and sly. He pretended to be pleased to see his nephew, embracing him like his own son, but in his heart he was wondering how best he might make use of his guest, who was in his eyes a homeless beggar. Jacob told Laban all that had happened to him, and about his dream. He stayed with his uncle for a month, and Laban saw that God had indeed blessed him. All his work was blessed with success, and Laban was anxious to keep this useful visitor for as long as possible.

Now Laban had two daughters, Rachel and Leah. Rachel, the younger girl, was tall, slim and beautiful. Her beauty was greater than that of Leah, her elder sister, who was quiet and shy. Jacob soon fell in love with Rachel, and Laban saw this. 'Why should you work here for nothing,' he said to Jacob. 'Tell me what wages you want.'

'I will work for Rachel,' Jacob replied, exactly as Laban had expected. 'After seven years you shall give her to me as my wife.'

'Very well,' Laban agreed, pleased with the cheap wages he would be expected to pay.

From that day onwards Jacob served Laban in order to earn Rachel's hand in marriage. Every morning he took his uncle's herds to pasture. In the daytime he was troubled by the heat, and at night by the frost. He sought out the best pastures and drove off the wild animals; but he loved Rachel, and the seven years passed like seven days.

After the seven years were up, Laban called all the people of the neighbourhood together and held a feast such as those that are given for weddings. He waited for Jacob to go to bed, then instead of Rachel he brought in Leah. In the dark Jacob could not see that he had been deceived. In the morning he found out his mistake, but it was too late. Leah had spent the night un-

der the same roof as he, and that meant that they were man and wife.

'It is not the custom here to marry off the younger daughter before the elder,' Laban told him, 'but you shall have Rachel still. I will give her to you as your second wife within a week, if you promise to serve me for another seven years.'

What was Jacob to do? He loved Rachel very much, and so he promised to do what Laban wanted. He carried on watching over his uncle's flocks. There were more and more sheep and goats in them, and Laban grew richer. Years went by.

In the meantime Jacob's family grew.

63 *Jacob's Tribulation*

Jacob enjoyed eleven sons and a daughter – all healthy and very beautiful children, a pleasure to behold. But one thing saddened Jacob. He was still working for Laban and had not earned anything for his family.

After fourteen years had passed, Jacob's service was at an end. 'Let me go,' he told his father-in-law, 'so that I may return to my own land. Before I came here your flocks were small, and now they stretch as far as the eye can see. God has blessed you on my account, and you should give me my wages, so that my wives and children may have something of their own.'

Laban did not like to hear this. He did not want either to lose Jacob or to part with any of his property. He hid his feel-

ings, and asked, 'What am I to give you?'

'Give me all your spotted sheep and goats,' Jacob replied. 'The white ones will be yours, and those with black spots mine.'

Laban frowned. It seemed to him that Jacob was asking too much, but he had an idea. He knew how he would trick Jacob, and he smiled.

'Very well,' he told Jacob. 'It shall be as you wish.'

The moment Jacob had left, Laban called his sons and went with them to his flocks. They set the pied and mottled sheep apart and made ready to take them to pastures which were several days away from there. All the animals which were

left had pure white fleece, and Laban chuckled with glee to think how he had made a fool of Jacob.

But God did not let Laban beguile Jacob. Jacob cut switches and peeled the bark off them in such a way that they had light and dark stripes. He put the switches in the troughs from which the animals drank. The animals who drank from these troughs eventually gave birth to striped and mottled young. Jacob was careful to let only the best animals drink from the troughs with the switches in them. He made the feeble goats and the weak ewes drink elsewhere. That way Laban was left with the weak creatures, and the strong ones were born to Jacob.

From that day onward his herds grew in size. Only a few years had passed, and with God's help Jacob had become a wealthy man. He had earned his wealth

Jacob's Tribulation

a hundred times over, but Laban's sons spoke ill of him, saying, 'He has robbed our father of everything he had.'

Jacob had another dream. 'Go quickly out of this land,' an angel of God told him. 'Go back to your father Isaac.'

The next day Jacob and his whole family prepared for the journey without telling Laban, who would be sure to stop them. Early in the morning he put his wives and children on camels and drove his flocks westwards, into the promised land of Canaan.

When Laban found out what had happened, he was filled with rage. He called his brothers and they went in pursuit of Jacob. For seven days Laban was at Jacob's heels, thinking only of vengeance. The night fell. Laban had a dream, in which God spoke to him. 'Take care,' He warned. 'Do not place any obstacles in Jacob's way.'

Even in his anger Laban dared not go against the will of God. When he caught up with Jacob and his family the next day, Laban decided to make a pact with Jacob. He promised Jacob friendship, and Jacob agreed to live in peace with Laban.

So, Jacob was able to rid himself of one pursuer, but his fears were not at an end. Laban had deceived him, but his brother, Esau, hated him. Laban had wished to rob him, while Esau wanted to kill him. Jacob had reached the borders of the land of Seir, where Esau lived. Jacob knew he would meet his brother, and he was afraid of him. 'Perhaps Esau's anger will pass if I send messengers to him,' thought Jacob. 'They shall tell him I want to live in peace.'

When the messengers returned they told Jacob fearfully, 'Esau is coming to meet you with four hundred men.'

Jacob was seized with fear. 'I shall have to keep the peace by offering Esau gifts,' he thought, and he sent more servants with hundreds of goats, sheep, cattle and camels. Then he divided his remaining flocks and servants into two camps. If one camp is slaughtered by Esau, then the other will survive, he supposed. When he had made these preparations for a meeting with his brother, he bowed his head and prayed. 'Dear God, God of my grandfather Abraham and my father Isaac,' he whispered, 'save me from Esau. Do not allow him to slay Rachel and Leah, and preserve my children.'

Darkness fell, but Jacob could not sleep. He rose up and quietly left the camp. He was quite alone, with only his worries to keep him company. Suddenly an angel of God appeared out of the dark in human form. He attacked Jacob and fought with him all night. Jacob was wounded. The stranger put his hip out of joint, so that Jacob limped, but he went on fighting. He gripped God's envoy until the morning star appeared.

'Let me go now,' the angel of God told him. 'Dawn is coming.'

'Not until you have blessed me,' Jacob replied.

At this the angel told him, 'You will no longer be known just as Jacob, but also as Israel, God's Warrior. You have fought before God and man like a nobleman, and you have not disgraced yourself.'

The Sun rose, and Jacob's fear suddenly left him. God's messenger had called him a noble warrior. He felt stronger. He was prepared to face Esau, even if his brother took up his sword.

A cloud of dust appeared on the horizon. Esau was drawing close, along with his four hundred warriors. Jacob walked towards them. He bowed to Esau seven times, and Esau went out to meet him, but his face was not clouded with anger. Esau came in peace. Throwing his arms round Jacob's neck, he kissed him, and the two of them wept tears of joy.

For many years Jacob had lived in a foreign land. He had fled in fear, and now he was returning happy. He had left alone, and he came back with a large family. He had nothing when he went, and was rich when he got back home. God had fulfilled His promise. He had not forsaken Jacob, but had lent him his strength.

Jacob's Tribulation

Joseph and his Brothers

Jacob grew old, and his sons became young men. Eleven of them had been born in Mesopotamia, but the twelfth, Benjamin, first saw the light of this world when Jacob was on his way back to the Promised Land. Benjamin's mother Rachel died giving birth to him, and this made Jacob love his youngest son even more. Joseph, to whom Rachel had given birth earlier, was equally close to his heart. He had no other sons by her. Now that they had lost their mother, Jacob treated them more kindly than their brothers, and the elder of the two, Joseph, became his trusted helper. To show his affection Jacob had a coat made for him out of brightly coloured fabric. Because the other sons did not receive such presents, they began to hate Joseph.

Joseph and his brothers tended the family's flocks. One day he had a dream. In it he and his brothers were reaping grain. While binding the ears into sheaves, Joseph's sheaf suddenly stood up. His brothers' sheaves walked around it and bowed to it with deference.

'Whatever can you be thinking?' his brothers asked angrily, when he told them of his dream. 'Do you suppose you are going to rule over us like a king?'

Not long after Joseph had his dream, he set out for the most distant of their pastures to take his brothers a message from their father. When they saw him coming, they began to speak about how they might kill him, but the eldest of them, Reuben, felt sorry for Joseph.

'Why should we spill our brother's blood?' he said. 'We will throw him into the well. He will never be able to get out.'

Reuben was secretly hoping to set Joseph free when the moment came, but the rest of the brothers wanted him to die. When he came up to them they seized him, tore off the cloak his father had given him, and without mercy threw him into the old well. Then they began to eat and drink merrily, giving their poor brother nothing. In the meantime Reuben went round with the flocks. At evening, when he returned, he was shocked: Joseph was no longer in the well.

While he had been on his rounds, a caravan of Midian merchants had arrived, carrying perfumed spices and swell smelling ointments from faraway Egypt.

'What use is it to us if Joseph dies,' one of the brothers had called out. 'Let us sell him to these merchants! That way we shall be rid of him, and shall have money into the bargain.'

The others agreed. Paying no heed to Joseph's cries or pleas, they sold him to the merchants. They dipped his coat in the blood of a goat, and afterwards they showed it to his father, telling him wild beasts had eaten his favourite son.

'Joseph is dead! My son is dead!' cried

Jacob, stricken with grief. So he mourned the death of his son, not knowing that Joseph was indeed still alive.

The Midian merchants took Jacob's son to the capital of the Egyptian empire and sold him in the slave market. He was bought by Potifar, the captain of the guard which protected the life of the Pharaoh, ruler of all Egypt. Potifar was a very noble man who had a big house and many slaves, but Joseph became his favourite. He soon learned to speak Egyptian and he was quick witted and clever. God looked with favour on everything he did, and whatever task Potifar gave him he completed to the utmost satisfaction. Potifar grew to trust Joseph more each day. First of all he made him steward of his house, and then his treasurer.

Now, Joseph was not only clever, he was also handsome. One day, as he was walking about his master's house as usual to see that all was in order, Potifar's wife stepped out to meet him.

'How handsome and skilful you are,' she said, with a smile. 'I should like such a husband as you, not an old man like Potifar.'

The woman thought Joseph would also begin to flatter her, but he said only, 'You belong to my master, whose feelings I care about. Why do you say these things?'

These words made Potifar's wife very angry. She, a noble woman, had taken a liking to Joseph, but he, a common slave, had the rudeness to refuse her friendship! 'You will be the worse for this, Joseph!' she hissed angrily, and suddenly she began to scream, as though she were being attacked. Potifar's servants came running from all sides. 'He wished to harm me!' she cried, pointing to Joseph. 'Throw him into prison. There he will have time to think about the wrong he has done me.'

Joseph tried in vain to convince Potifar of his innocence. The commander of the royal guard believed his wife's lies, and had Joseph thrown into prison. Deep under the ground in a dungeon which was dark and lonely, he recalled his wicked brothers, who had brought about his misfortune. At first he hoped he might be taken before a court, so that he could prove his innocence, but as the days went by he realized he had already been sentenced without a hearing. God did not abandon Joseph in his hour of need, however. Just as Potifar had shown favour to him, so in time he became friends with the commander of the prison. Within two or three years he had handed over all the prisoners to Joseph's charge. Joseph lived in a more comfortable cell, and in spite of all his troubles, his life became easier to bear.

When Joseph had been in prison for ten years, for some reason or other, two of the Pharaoh's servants were locked up too. They were the head waiter at the palace, who chose the Pharaoh's drinks and served him at table, and the chief baker, who baked the Pharaoh's bread and cakes. While the two of them were waiting to hear their judgement, Joseph, on the orders of the commander of the prison, acted as their servant. One day, he came upon

the two men looking sad and ill at ease.

'What is wrong?' he asked.

'We both had strange dreams, and do not know how to explain them,' the waiter and the baker told him.

'God willing, I will explain your dreams,' Joseph replied. 'Tell me about them!'

The waiter was the first to speak. 'I saw a vine with three shoots. The grapes ripened suddenly, and I picked them, pressed the juice into a cup, and gave it to the Pharaoh.'

'You have nothing to fear,' Joseph told him. 'Those three shoots were three days. When they have passed, the Pharaoh will take you back into his palace and you will serve him as before.'

Seeing that Joseph had comforted the waiter, the baker quickly told his own dream. 'I dreamed I was carrying on my head three baskets of bread for the Pharaoh. Suddenly the birds came along and began to peck away at the top basket.'

'The three baskets,' Joseph said, 'are also three days. On the third day the Pharaoh will have you put to death. You will hang and the birds will peck your flesh.'

The waiter and the baker counted the days anxiously. On the third day the Pharaoh celebrated his birthday. He ate, he drank, and he remembered the waiter and the baker. 'Let all hear my judgement,' he cried. 'I forgive the waiter his crime. He shall serve me again. As for the baker, he shall be hanged.'

So it was that what Joseph had foretold came true. Before the waiter left prison, he promised Joseph he would speak to the Pharaoh on his behalf. The moment he was out of gaol, though, he forgot all about poor Joseph. So the innocent Joseph continued to spend his days in prison, and the waiter enjoyed the Pharaoh's favour.

He would never have remembered Joseph at all, if the Pharaoh had not strange dreams some years later. His most respected sages and soothsayers tried to interpret them for him, but they were not able to. Then the waiter said to the Pharaoh, 'When I was in prison with the chief baker, we were served by a young man from a faraway country. One night, the baker and I had dreams, which the man explained exactly.'

The Pharaoh sent for Joseph at once. Firstly Joseph washed and cut his hair. Then he was given fine clothes, and for the first time in many years he came out of the dungeons into the light of day. When he came before the ruler of Egypt, the Pharaoh said to him, 'I had a dream. Seven beautiful, well-fed cows stepped out of the River Nile and began grazing on the banks. Behind them seven lean cows, all skin and bone, stepped out and ate the fat ones. I was startled and woke up. Then I fell asleep again, and had another dream. This time I saw a stalk of grain on which there were seven full, fat ears of grain. Next to

them were seven empty ears, and they swallowed up the full ones. What does this mean?'

'This is one and the same dream,' Joseph told him. 'The seven fat cows and the

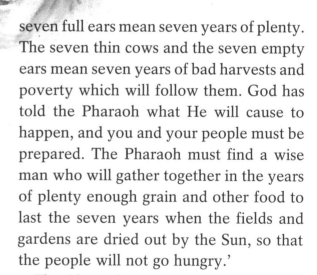

seven full ears mean seven years of plenty. The seven thin cows and the seven empty ears mean seven years of bad harvests and poverty which will follow them. God has told the Pharaoh what He will cause to happen, and you and your people must be prepared. The Pharaoh must find a wise man who will gather together in the years of plenty enough grain and other food to last the seven years when the fields and gardens are dried out by the Sun, so that the people will not go hungry.'

The Pharaoh and his counsellors were pleased with these words. 'God speaks to you,' the Pharaoh said to Joseph. 'Who could be a better steward for my kingdom?' Then the Pharaoh took off his ring and gave it to Joseph. He hung a golden chain around his neck as a sign of the high office he held, and gave Joseph a suit of the finest clothes.

That day Joseph became the second most powerful man in Egypt. In time he married a girl from a noble family and they had two sons, Manasseh and Ephraim. Joseph rode the length and breadth of the land and had granaries built everywhere, for the seven years of plenty had begun. Huge quantities of grain were harvested. The granaries were filled to overflowing.

Then came the years of great famine. The fields, gardens and vineyards ceased to be fruitful, and hunger reigned in all the surrounding lands. Only in Egypt was there plenty. The people went to Joseph, and he gave them grain.

In the land of Canaan, where Joseph's father Jacob and his brothers lived, there was also famine. Jacob called together his sons and told them, 'Go to Egypt and buy corn, so that we do not die of hunger.'

The brothers saddled their asses and set out. All of them went except for the youngest, Benjamin, whom their father did not want to leave home. 'Rachel gave me two sons,' he thought. 'I have lost Joseph, but nothing must happen to Benjamin.'

After a long trek, Jacob's ten sons reached the capital city of the Egyptian empire. Because people told him that the Pharaoh's steward distributed grain, they set out for his palace. They had never seen

such splendour. When they saw the steward, they bowed low to him, but none of them suspected that the man in the magnificent robes of an Egyptian nobleman might be their brother. Joseph, however, recognized his brothers at once. He remembered his dream long ago when his brothers' sheaves had bowed to him, and recalled the hard times he had suffered because of them. Looking at them sternly, he asked, 'Who are you?'

'We come from the land of Canaan, and we should like to buy grain,' they said.

'You are lying,' Joseph cried. 'You are spies, and you have come to do evil!'

The brothers swore that they meant no harm, and told of their old father, whom they had left at home with their youngest brother, and of the hunger which had brought them to Egypt. 'I will test you to see if you are speaking the truth,' said Joseph. 'One of you must return and bring your youngest brother. If he comes, then I will believe you.'

He had the rest of them bound and thrown into prison, so that they might see how unpleasant it had been for him to suffer when he had done no wrong.

'We harmed Joseph, and now we are being punished for it,' the brothers said. 'He asked us for mercy, but we showed him none.'

Tears came to Joseph's eyes, but he hid his feelings and had the brothers brought to him again. 'I will lessen your suffering,' he told them. 'It shall be enough for one of you to remain in prison. He will stay

Joseph and his Brothers

there until the rest return with the youngest brother.'

Joseph signalled to the guards and they led away Simeon, the second eldest son. In the meantime the brothers' sacks had been filled with grain. Joseph ordered the silver with which the brothers had paid to be put in the sacks, too, without telling them. At dawn they set off for their home. They had plenty of food with them, but they were sad, none the less. They felt sorry for having harmed Joseph and were fearful for Simeon. When they found the silver in their sacks, their fear grew even stronger. 'When we go back to Egypt, they will consider us thieves,' they thought.

Jacob would not hear of them going back again. 'I have lost Joseph, and Simeon is no longer here. Now you are asking me to let Benjamin go?!' he cried out.

The famine in the land of Canaan worsened, and one day there was not a grain of corn left in the sacks. 'Father,' said the brother named Judah, 'if we do not buy grain in Egypt, we will die of hunger. We cannot go without Benjamin. I will take charge of him. If I do not bring him home again, I shall be guilty before you.'

What was Jacob to do? Unhappily he agreed, and sent Benjamin with the rest of his sons. As Jacob had advised them, they took back to Egypt the silver they had found in their sacks, along with gifts for the steward of the empire and enough silver to pay for more corn.

When Joseph saw that his brothers had brought Benjamin with them, he ordered his steward to make ready good food, and led the travellers into the palace. The brothers were afraid. 'Now they are going to accuse us of stealing the silver,' they thought. They quickly returned it to Joseph's steward, but he gave it back saying, 'The God of you and your fathers gave you that silver. You owe nothing.'

The brothers were surprised, and their surprise soon gave way to joy at being reunited with their brother Simeon. Before long Joseph came to the palace, too. The brothers gave him the presents they had brought, and Joseph invited them to the table. He feasted them as if they were his best friends, asking about their father, and was attentive and kind to them. Afterwards he gave them rich presents, but to Benjamin, his own brother, he gave five times as much as to the others. Joseph saw how his brothers had changed; he saw the love with which they helped their father and each other. He wished he could embrace them, but he wanted to test them one more time, so he still did not tell them who he was.

While the brothers were eating, Joseph called his steward and told him his plan: 'Fill my brothers' sacks full of corn and put their silver in them; in the youngest brother's sack put my own silver goblet.'

The steward did as he was told, and the brothers set off home again. They had not got far beyond the city when the steward caught up with them and called out to them in a stern tone, just as his master had told him, 'How could you reward good with evil? One of you has stolen my master's silver goblet.'

'We should not dare to do such a thing,' the brothers replied. 'We wanted to return even the silver which was in our sacks the last time. You may search our baggage. Let he in whose things you find the goblet die, and the rest become slaves of your master.'

The brothers took the sacks down from their asses and untied them. Ten of them were filled with grain and silver, but in the eleventh, that belonging to Benjamin, there was a silver goblet as well. None of the brothers knew how it had happened. In tears and in fear they returned to the city and came before Joseph.

'What a crime you have committed!' cried Joseph. 'Do you not know that I find everything out? The thief will stay here as a slave; the rest of you must leave!'

Then Judah came forward. He was the one who had once suggested that they sell

Joseph to the Midian merchants. Now he fell on his knees before Joseph, pleading, 'Lord, please listen to what I have to say. We have already told you that we have an old father. He had two wives. One of them, Rachel, died long ago, leaving him two sons. The first was torn apart by wild animals, while the second, a child born when our father was an old man, is now to become your slave. Our father did not want to allow the youngest son to leave home, and I have pledged my life to bring the boy home. If Benjamin does not return, our father will die of grief. Allow me to serve you instead of my brother.'

Joseph could no longer hide his feelings. He sent out all of his Egyptian servants and cried, 'I am your brother Joseph, whom you sold into Egypt! God sent me here before you, so that our father's house would not die of hunger.'

The brothers were so surprised that they could barely speak. It was only when Joseph embraced them that they took courage. They wept with joy to see their brother again.

Soon the news of this strange reunion spread throughout the city. Even the Pharaoh heard about it. 'Tell your brothers to take waggons and to bring their wives, children and your old father from the land of Canaan,' he said to Joseph.

Before very long Joseph met his father again after many years.

'Now I can die in peace, since I have seen you, and know you are alive,' Jacob said, weeping tears of thankfulness.

Jacob lived on for many more years, however, and he and his children were given the fertile part of Egypt called Goshen, where they settled together in contentment and plenty.

Moses

Jacob was dead, and so were all his sons, but their descendants lived on. Boys and girls grew up and married, and in time there were quite a number of Israelites living in Egypt. The Pharaoh who had shown great favour to Joseph was also long dead. The land was ruled by new lords, and Joseph's deeds had begun to be forgotten.

One day a new Pharaoh came to the throne; one who had not even heard of Joseph and all his good work. The Pharaoh was envious of the Israelites because they were a strong and successful people. 'There are too many of these outlanders here,' he thought. 'If we were to be attacked by an enemy, they would be sure to join forces with him. I will make them slaves, so that they will know how powerful I am.'

The Pharaoh put soldiers and guards in charge of the Israelites, who were put to work as slaves. From dawn until dusk Jacob's people toiled for the Pharaoh. They built the cities of Pithom and Rameses, but still the Pharaoh was not satisfied. He hoped that hard labour would break the spirit of the children of Israel; he wanted them to die of exhaustion. But the Israelites did not waver. There were no fewer of them than before, and so the Pharaoh gave a terrible order. 'Every boy born to the Israelites shall be thrown into the Nile to drown,' he ordered the Egyptians. 'The girls shall be spared.'

During this time of terrible hardship a son was born to a certain Israeli woman who was a daughter of the house of Levi. She hid him for three months, but that was as long as she dared. So she wove a small basket out of reeds, put the child in it, and, with faith in God, put the basket on the banks of the Nile.

Unseen, the baby's elder sister hid in the reeds and watched what would happen. Before long Pharaoh's daughter came by. She and her servants had come to bathe in the river, but before they went into the water they saw the basket with the beautiful boy child in it. The princess felt great pity for the tiny baby.

'He is a child of Israel,' she thought, 'and he should be drowned. Surely it does not matter if this one boy is spared. I will let him live.'

At that moment the boy's sister stepped out of the reeds. 'Am I to call an Israeli woman to nurse the boy?' she asked the Pharaoh's daughter.

'Yes, go and find someone to look after him,' said the princess.

So the girl ran to fetch her mother, and the little boy went home that day.

'When the child has grown a little, I will bring him to you,' his mother told the princess.

The Pharaoh's daughter agreed, and the mother looked after her own child. She rocked him in her arms and comforted him, thanking God for saving him.

When the boy grew bigger, the Pharaoh's daughter adopted him as her own son. She called him 'Moses' which means *pulled out*, because she had rescued him from drowning in the Nile. In the Pharaoh's house Moses learned everything which a child from a noble family should know. Even though he was not with her, he did not forget his own mother, and he knew he belonged with the children of Israel, who suffered under the cruelty of the Egyptians. One day Moses went out of the palace to see for himself the work his brothers had to do. Before he had gone far, he caught sight of an Egyptian slave-driver beating an Israelite. Moses went to the poor man's aid. Seeing there was no one else around, he killed the Egyptian and buried the body in the sand. He then returned to the palace.

The next day Moses went out again. Hearing raised voices, he came upon two Israelites in the middle of a heated argument.

'What are you doing?' Moses shouted at the one who was in the wrong.

The man only scowled at him and said, 'Who made you my master? Do you want to kill me, as you killed the Egyptian?'

took flight. It was only just in time. The Pharaoh had already heard about what Moses had done, and had sent soldiers to kill him. They searched in vain, however, for Moses was nowhere to be found. He had left Egypt in secret, and set out for the land of Midian, beyond the borders of the Pharaoh's empire.

Tired from his long journey, he stopped and sat down beside a well, which was on the edge of a certain town. As he sat there, seven sisters came by to draw water for their flocks. They let down their buckets into the cool water, but before the animals had had time to drink, some shepherds came by and drove the girls away. Moses could not bear to see such an unfair act, and he stood up, and gave the girls' animals water with his own hands.

The girls' father was a well-respected man, the Midian priest Jethro. When his daughters told him what Moses had done, he invited the young man to his house. Moses was received as an honoured guest, and he stayed on in the house. After some time Jethro gave Moses his daughter, Zipporah, as his wife but Moses was not happy. What good was all this when he knew that his brothers were suffering in Egypt? How could he take pleasure in his son Gershom, when Israelite mothers were mourning their sons whom the Egyptians drowned? The evil Pharaoh had since died, but his successor hated the people of Israel even more.

God heard their cries and remembered his promise to Abraham, Isaac and Jacob.

Moses became frightened. 'I will be found out,' he thought. 'I shall have to run away, or the Pharaoh will have me exe-cuted.'

Leaving the two men to their fate, he

'I will save my people,' God said. 'I will release them from slavery, and Moses will be their leader.'

In the meantime, Moses pastured his father-in-law's sheep. One day, when he took them as far as the holy mountain Horeb, he saw a strange sight. One of the bushes caught fire in front of him, burning with a bright flame. For some reason the wood did not turn to ashes. Wishing to see why this was so, Moses went closer, but suddenly God spoke to him from out of the fire. 'Moses, I am here. Do not come any nearer,' said God. 'Take your sandals from your feet, Moses, for you stand on holy ground.'

Moses hid his face because he was afraid to look at God, and God went on speaking.

'I am the God of Abraham, the God of Isaac, and the God of Jacob,' He said. 'I know the suffering your people have had to face in Egypt, and I will not let it go on any longer. You must go to the Pharaoh to ask him to let you bring my people out of Egypt. You will lead them to the land filled with milk and honey I have promised.'

'I am too lowly to do such work,' said Moses. 'How could the Pharaoh do as I ask him? Not even my own people will believe me. They will say, "You are lying. You have not seen the Lord."'

Then God said, 'Throw your staff on the ground.'

Moses threw down his staff, and it changed into a snake.

'Pick it up by the tail,' said God.

Moses picked the snake up by its tail, and it changed back into a staff.

'Now put your hand on to your breast underneath your clothes,' God told him.

Moses did as he was told, and when he drew it out again, it was weak and bloodless, as white as snow. He put his hand back under his clothing, and when he drew it out again, its strength had been restored.

'If my people do not believe the first sign,' God told him, 'they will believe the second. If they do not believe the second sign either, and will not follow you, take some water from the Nile. Pour it on to dry ground, and it will turn into blood.'

Moses was still not sure, and he said to God, 'Lord, I am not a good speaker. My tongue is not a nimble one. How am I to speak to the Pharaoh?'

God replied, 'Who gave people their mouths? Is it not through my will that they speak? Go to the Pharaoh. Aaron, your brother, will go with you. He has a way with words. I will stand by you and tell you what do do.'

After he had heard these words, Moses waited no longer. He picked up the staff of God and set off back into Egypt, the land of slavery. Neither the Pharaoh nor Moses' people had any idea what was being prepared. The hour of deliverance was at hand.

Moses

The Israelites in Egypt

Moses took the road to Egypt. In a desert scorched by the Sun, not far from the Holy Mountain, he met his brother Aaron. The pair of them embraced each other joyously, and went on their way together. Even though they did not radiate light like the heavenly angels, they were still God's messengers. They crossed the borders of the Egyptian empire in secret and called a meeting of the elders of the Israelites.

'God has taken pity on you,' Aaron told the down-hearted sages. 'He has sent us to lead you out of Egyptian slavery.'

At these words Moses turned his staff into a snake and the snake back into a staff. Then he took a little water from the Nile and poured it on to the ground. It turned to blood.

When the elders of the people saw what power God had given to Moses, they fell on their knees before the two brothers, believing that they had been sent by Him.

Moses and Aaron went before the Pharaoh. The ruler of all Egypt looked down upon them with great arrogance from his golden throne, but Moses and Aaron knew that their God was more powerful than this earthly ruler. 'The Lord has spoken,' they told the Pharaoh. 'Let my people go,

so that they may hold a ceremony in my honour out in the desert.'

'What Lord is this I am supposed to obey?' roared the Pharaoh. 'I will not release my slaves!'

So he called the soldiers and guards who had charge of the Israelites and ordered them to treat the slaves more cruelly than ever. The straw that they usually had for mixing with clay to make bricks was no longer provided by the Egyptians. Now the Israelites had to go into the fields themselves to collect it. Although they collected it as quickly as they could, it took much longer to make the bricks because of the time they lost, and so they could not make as many. Then their slave-drivers punished them. The Israelites wept and wailed. When they saw Moses and Aaron, they complained bitterly, 'You spoke ill of us in front of the Pharaoh. Now we are worse off than ever. We shall all die here!'

God spoke to Moses. 'Do not worry,' He told him. 'I will make the Pharaoh set my people free. Do as I tell you.'

The next morning Moses waited for the Pharaoh on the banks of the Nile. When the ruler of Egypt came up to the river, Moses spoke to the Pharaoh as God had told him to do. 'You have not listened to the God of Israel,' he said, 'and have not set His people free. Now you will witness his power.'

No sooner had Moses finished speaking, than Aaron struck the staff of God against the water of the Nile, and it turned to blood. The fish died, the water stank, and

83

the Egyptians could not bathe in the river. The Egyptian magicians were also able to turn water to blood, so the Pharaoh was still not convinced of the power of God. So God again spoke to Moses and Aaron. 'Tell the Pharaoh again to free my people. If he does not obey this time, I will send a plague of frogs upon Egypt.'

The Pharaoh listened to what God's messengers had to say, but did not do as they asked. So Aaron drew his staff over the lakes and springs. In an instant the whole of the land of Egypt was covered in frogs. They filled fields and houses, crawling into the houses of the people, even into their beds and into the bowls in which the bread was kneaded. The Pharaoh's magicians also conjured up frogs. When it came to getting rid of the frogs sent by God, however, their magic was useless. Thousands of frogs leapt from the River Nile, crawling over the Pharaoh and his servants. Then the Pharaoh sent for Moses and Aaron. 'Tell your God to take away the frogs,' he begged. 'Then I will let His people go.'

So Moses asked the Lord to have mercy on the Egyptians, and God caused the frogs to die. The people gathered them up in heaps and the land stank. Even this sign did not convince the Pharaoh of the power of God. He did not keep his promise, and made the Israelites work on as slaves. God saw that the Pharaoh was not going to give way, and He sent a plague of mosquitoes. There were more of them than there are grains of dust, and they settled in clouds on man and beast. This was more than the Egyptian magicians were able to do and they spoke to the Pharaoh. 'This is the finger of God,' they told him, fearfully. The proud Pharaoh again took no notice of their warning. He did not humble himself before God, and still kept the Israelites as slaves. So God sent a fourth plague upon the Egyptians. Thick clouds of flies descended on the whole land. They got into Pharaoh's house, and into the houses of his servants. They covered the whole land of Egypt. The only part of the land which was not touched was the land of Goshen where the Israelites lived. The Pharaoh had to ask Moses for help. 'I will set the Israelites free, so that they may make a sacrifice to your God in the desert,' he said. 'Only send the flies away.'

Moses asked the Lord, and the flies ceased to torment the land, but the moment they had gone, the Pharaoh went back on his word. He did not obey God's word, and once more refused to set the Israelites free. So God sent another plague to the Pharaoh. All the farm animals in the land became sick. Horses, asses and camels died in their thousands. Only the animals belonging to the Israelites were not affected. Still the Pharaoh had not learnt his lesson, so God's sixth blow fell. Festering sores appeared on the bodies of the Egyptians and their animals. Even the Pharaoh's magicians were covered in them from head to foot. Still the Pharaoh remained unmoved. God struck harder than ever. 'Hold your staff up to heaven,' He said to Moses. Moses did as God asked, and God sent terrible rains and hailstorms. Lightning streaked across the skies, and thunder shook the ground. The Egyptians had never before seen such destruction. The crops were flattened in the fields, and hailstones battered men and beasts to death. Only the land where the Israelites lived remained calm and whole. There the Sun shone brightly, and there was no destruction. The Pharaoh saw what was happening to his land, and he called Moses and Aaron. 'Tell God to stop the hail,' he begged them. 'I will free your people. They need stay here no longer.'

So Moses raised his hands to the Lord and prayed. The hailstorms stopped at once, but the Pharaoh did not set the Israelites free.

'I will work more wonders,' God told Moses. 'If the Pharaoh does not set my people free, I will bring a plague of locusts. They will cover the whole land, and will devour what has been left by hail.'

When the Pharaoh's servants heard about this, they ran to their master. 'Let the Israelites go,' they cried. 'Egypt will be destroyed because of them.'

The Pharaoh still did not want to give way. 'Only the menfolk may go,' he declared.

85

'The women and children must stay here.'

No sooner had the Pharaoh finished speaking than Moses turned his staff towards the land of Egypt. At this signal, God sent an easterly wind. It blew all day and all night, and with it came millions of locusts. They ate all the fruits of the earth and the trees, and not a patch of greenery was left in the land of Egypt. The Pharaoh sent for Moses and Aaron at once. 'Let your God take away this plague,' he told them. 'Let me be punished no more!'

God heard the Pharaoh's words, and changed the direction of the wind. A powerful gust of wind seized the locusts and hurled them all into the Red Sea, beyond the borders of the Egyptian empire. Still the Pharaoh's heart was not softened. When the plague had passed, he treated the Israelites just as cruelly as ever. So God spoke to Moses once again. 'Hold out your hand to Heaven,' He told him, 'and the land of Egypt shall be covered in darkness.'

Moses raised his right hand, and a great darkness fell upon the land of Egypt. For three days the Egyptians could see nothing. It was as though they were blind. No one came out of his house in all that time. Even inside it was dark, but in the homes of the Israelites there was light. The frightened Pharaoh sent for Moses. 'You and your people must leave,' he told him. 'Leave behind only your animals.'

'We will all go,' Moses told him firmly. 'Our men, women, and children, and all our herds.'

This made Pharaoh angry. 'Get out of my sight!' he shouted at Moses. 'I will let no one go. If you come here again, you shall die!'

When He heard these words, God said to Moses, 'The Pharaoh of Egypt shall suffer one more blow, and after that he will let you go. At midnight I will move throughout the land of Egypt. I will cause all the firstborn sons to die, from the Pharaoh's to that of the humblest servant. I will save the firstborn of the Israelites. You shall hold a celebration in my honour tonight. Eat a roast lamb with bitter herbs, and bake bread without yeast. Use the blood of the lamb to paint the lintels and doorposts of your houses. When I strike Egypt, I will see where your houses are, and your children will be saved.'

Exactly at midnight, God struck dead the firstborn of all the houses in Egypt. A great wail went up throughout Egypt, as there was no Egyptian house where someone did not die. The sound of crying and lamenting woke up the Pharaoh. That same night he called Moses and Aaron and begged plaintively, 'Go. Go, and take with you your wives and your children, and your herds as well. Serve the Lord as you wish, or we shall all die.'

The Israelites had already made preparations. That night none of them had slept. When dusk fell, they had eaten the lamb, as God had ordered. They had their sandals on their feet, and they held staffs in their hands. The sign they made on their doors had saved them from the mighty hand of God, and now they all waited for the signal from Moses. At last they set off. In the daytime the messenger of God went in front of them wrapped in a pillar of cloud, and at night it was a pillar of fire. The Israelites set out on the long journey to the Promised Land, and God was their protector. Meanwhile, Egypt was filled with mourning. The Egyptians grieved for their dead, but Pharaoh was already making plans for vengeance. 'It was foolish of me to let the Israelites go,' he thought. 'Who will do the work of the slaves?'

The Pharaoh roused his people into action, and sent the army in pursuit of the Israelites. He had his own chariot harnessed up, and set out after them with another six hundred chariots containing fully armed warriors. The Israelites had reached the banks of the Red Sea and had pitched their camp on its banks.

Now they saw the Pharaoh's army appear on the horizon. The Israelites became frightened. 'Because there were no graves for us in Egypt, have you led us out into the desert to die?' they said to Moses. 'It would have been better to remain there as slaves.'

Moses only said, 'Do not be afraid. The Lord will fight on our side. Stand and watch.'

The Pharaoh's chariots and horsemen were fast approaching. Suddenly, the mes-

senger of the Lord, wrapped in cloud, placed himself between the camp of the Israelites and the Egyptians. The Egyptian army was covered in darkness, but the Israelites had light enough. Then God spoke to Moses. 'Hold your staff out over the sea,' He said.

The moment Moses did this the Lord sent an easterly wind over the Red Sea. It blew all night, and divided the water into two halves, leaving dry land in between them. The Israelites walked along the bed of the sea, with water towering on both sides like two huge walls.

Eager for victory, the Egyptians set off after the fugitives. Their drawn swords gleamed in the sunlight, and the vision of what seemed like an easy prey drove them onward. Then God looked down on the Pharaoh's soldiers, and caused confusion to break out in the Egyptian army. The warriors could not control their horses, and the wheels of their chariots broke off. The Egyptians turned and began to run away. 'God is on the side of Israel!' they cried in terror.

It was too late. Once again, Moses reached out his hand over the sea, and the walls of water crashed down on the Egyptians. The proud Pharaoh and all his soldiers were drowned and left lying like stones on the sea bed.

The Israelites in Egypt

In the Desert

God led His people into the Promised Land. He knew them well, so He did not take them by the shortest route through the land of the Palestinians, who were awesome warriors. 'The Israelites have done enough fighting,' thought God. 'Let them go around Palestine and be saved from death.'

So the Israelites went through the desert of Shur, an endless stretch of hot sand. They walked for three days without finding water. Men, women and children were thirsty, longing for a draught of cool water. At last they came to Marah where they found a spring.

When they tasted the water, however, their joy turned to disappointment. 'It is bitter,' they murmured. 'We cannot drink it. What shall we drink?'

Moses prayed to the Lord, and the Lord showed him a tree. Moses threw the tree into the bitter water, and the water became sweet and fit to drink. God said to Moses, 'I will test your people many more times, so that they learn not to waver in the face of misfortune, but to trust in my

power. Tell them to obey my orders, and I will lead them safely to the Promised Land.'

Soon after this the Israelites arrived in Elim. It was a beautiful place. Water gushed from twelve springs, and seventy palm trees gently rustled in the wind. The Israelites saw with their own eyes how well God guided them, but still some of them doubted. 'Is God with us, or isn't He?' they asked, and they complained to Moses whenever anything went wrong.

In the second month after the Israelites left their life of slavery in Egypt, they arrived in the desert of Sinai. Here, too, the Sun blazed down mercilessly, and the travellers' feet sank into the hot sand. 'If only God had destroyed us in the land of Egypt,' the complaining ones cried. 'There we sat over pots of meat, and ate our fill of bread. Now Moses and Aaron have brought us out into the desert to die of hunger!'

How soon the Israelites had forgotten their times of hardship in Egypt! How quickly their sufferings in slavery had

In the Desert

been wiped from their minds! Their bodies were covered in scars from the beatings they had received, but they seemed to prefer this to the trials sent them by the Lord. God heard the complaints of the Israelites, and He said to Moses, 'I will look after you, I will give you meat and bread.'

When evening came a flock of quails landed in the camp of the Israelites. There were so many of them that people were able to eat their fill. Then, towards morning, a strange type of dew descended. When the dew had gone there remained small round things where it had been. This was the bread the Lord had promised them. The Israelites called it *manna,* and it was white like coriander seeds and tasted like wafers made with honey. Moses told them how to eat it.

'This is the word of God, who brought you out of the land of Egypt,' He said. 'Take as much manna as you need to stem your hunger. Do not gather more than you can eat. What you do not eat will be eaten by worms. Only on the sixth day you should gather manna for the seventh day, the day of rest. On that day you should not either cook or bake, and you must do no work. If you do as God tells you, whatever you gather on the sixth day, will remain fresh for the Sabbath and will not go bad.'

Once again there were people among the Israelites who doubted the word of God. They gathered more manna than they needed on ordinary days, and they went out to gather it on the seventh day, too. They took no notice of the fact that the food they stored was bad the next day, nor that they found no manna on the Sabbath. They tried the patience of God and He became angry. 'How long will these people refuse to obey my commandments?' He said to Moses.

Moses did not know what to do. There were those among his people who kept losing faith in the power of God, and the

grumblers complained all the time. Now the Israelites arrived in Rephidim. Again they had nothing to drink, and they turned on Moses angrily, shouting, 'Give us water! Our children and our cattle are dying of thirst.'

'Why do you argue with me?' Moses asked, sadly. 'Why are you trying the patience of God?'

Moses was distraught, and he prayed to the Lord. 'God,' he said, 'what shall I do? The people are almost ready to stone me to death.'

'Take the staff I gave you,' God answered, 'Go with the elders of the Israelites to Mount Horeb. I will be standing nearby, but no one will see me. Strike the rocks with your staff, and water will come out.'

No one had ever seen or heard of such a miracle, so the Israelites waited expectantly to see what would happen. Moses raised God's staff and struck the rock. In an instant water began to pour out from it. Now there was no doubt. God was with Israel, and Moses was His chosen prophet.

In the Desert

The Laws of God

Three months after the Israelites left Egypt they arrived in the desert of Sinai. In the night they camped beneath a tall mountain. They all lay down to sleep, except Moses, who stayed awake. He went up to the mountain, to get nearer to God, and as the Israelites slept, God spoke to him.

'Tell the Israelites they are not to forget the wonderful deeds I performed in Egypt,' He said. 'I led you out of slavery, as though I were carrying you on the wings of an eagle. I brought you to me. Now, if you obey me, you shall become my chosen people, the only one of all nations I have created. Keep my laws and I will make you a blessed nation.'

In the morning, as soon as the Israelites woke up, Moses told them about what God had said. All of those who were in the camp, men, women and children, called out with one voice, 'We will do what God has told us to.'

When God heard this, he told Moses, 'Let everyone get ready for the day after tomorrow. They should make themselves free from sin, and wash their clothes. On the third day I will go on to Mount Sinai, which stands in front of you. All the people will see this, but no one must touch the mountain. No one may come near until they hear the trumpet sound. Anyone who disobeys will die!'

At dawn on the third day the sky became dark and there was a terrible crash of thunder, so loud that the mountain shook. The sky was streaked with lightning and the mountain was engulfed by thick cloud. The trumpet began to sound and it was so loud that they stood back and shook with fear. Moses brought his people out of the camp to meet with God and they stood at the foot of the mountain. Fire gushed from the mountain and the whole mountain shook. The trumpet sounded even louder and God came down upon the mountain and called Moses up to meet him. God spoke to Moses but Moses could not see Him. His voice came out of the fire, sounding out on all sides and booming across the land. All the Israelites heard Him. They heard the commandments of the Lord, which He called His law.

God said, 'I am your Lord, your God, who has brought you out of Egypt, out of slavery.

You must not worship other gods. You must not make pictures or statues of gods.

You must not bow down to an image of anything that is in the sky, on Earth or in the ocean, nor may you serve such things.

You must not use God's name for any other reason than talking about the true God.

You must have a day of rest, a holy day. Work for six days, but the seventh day is God's, a day of rest. You must not do any work then, nor must anyone in your house.

Respect your mother and father, so that you may live long and be prosperous.

You must not kill.

A man shall be faithful to his wife, and a woman to her husband.

You must not steal.

You must not bear false witness.

You must not envy those around you what they possess.'

When the people heard the voice of God, coming out of the fire, they began shouting to Moses, 'The Lord God had

shown us His glory and greatness. But He should not speak to us any longer, in case we are swallowed up by his fire and destroyed. Speak to God alone. Hear what He has to say, and then tell us about it.'

Moses said to them, 'God has come to you so that you will be afraid of Him, and will not commit any more sins. He loved Abraham, Isaac, Jacob and all their descendants. He led you out of Egypt, and He will give you the land He promised to your forefathers. Remember that He is the Lord of the Heavens above and the Earth

below, and no other. You must love God with all your heart and soul. Teach your children the laws you have heard, and be grateful to God. For He is merciful to those who love Him and obey His commandments, but those who do not love and obey Him will be punished.'

Then Moses went closer to the cloud at the summit of Mount Sinai, and God's cloud covered him up. Moses stayed on the mountain for forty days and nights, and all that time he had nothing to eat or drink. God spoke to him about His laws, and He taught Moses justice and righteousness. No one in the whole land had ever heard more noble words. God Himself wrote them down on stone tablets; He placed these tablets, containing an agreement between Him and men, in Moses's hands. God made a contract with men which bound them to obey His teaching. He gave it to the Israelites as a gift, so that God's truth would be with them always on their long journey.

The Laws of God

Balaam Blesses Israel

When God spoke to Moses on Mount Sinai, He showed him His holy dwelling place. 'Let the Israelites build me a tabernacle fit for their Lord,' He said, 'and I will live in their hearts and minds.'

So the Israelites made a tabernacle which was a place to worship God, as He asked. They made it exactly according to God's instructions, so that it could be carried around from place to place. It was fashioned from precious acacia wood, pure gold, and embroidered cloth. Inside the tabernacle they kept the chest called the Ark of the Covenant. In it were the tablets on which were written God's laws, which were given to Moses on Mount Sinai. Two cherubim fashioned in gold guarded over it; they were neither man nor beast, and their wings were raised towards Heaven.

It was in this place steeped in darkness, that God would meet Moses. God spoke to Moses and Moses told the Israelites what God wanted them to do.

On the day the tabernacle was finished, the cloud of God appeared above it and covered it up. In the night it shone with a fiery glow, and in the daytime it rose up and showed the Israelites the way. Whenever the cloud moved, the Israelites trav-elled on. When the cloud stopped, they made camp. God was with His people. With His help the Israelites defeated the powerful King Arad of Canaan; they won victories over Sihon, king of the Amorites, and Og, the king of Bashan. No one who went into battle with the Israelites was able to stand up to them. So one day they arrived on the borders of the kingdom of Moab, close to the Promised Land.

Balak, king of Moab, was very much afraid of the Israelites. He knew that God had given them immense strength, and he had heard how they had left Egypt in triumph, and how they had defeated the neighbouring kings. 'They are powerful because their God is powerful,' he thought to himself. 'I must first of all bring God's plans to nothing, then the Israelites will not be able to stand up to me.'

Balak already had a plan. In the neighbouring kingdom, in the city of Pethor, there lived a man called Balaam, a famous soothsayer and seer. Whoever was blessed by Balaam met with good fortune, but whoever was cursed by him had his fate sealed.

Balak sent noble messengers to see Balaam. They gave him Balak's message, but Balaam knew of the Creator's might, and he said to them, 'Stay here overnight. The Lord will speak to me in the night. Then I will tell you if I can help you or not.'

When Balaam fell asleep, he heard God's voice, 'Do not go with Balak's men,' He said. 'Do not curse my people, because they are blessed.'

In the morning Balaam told the messengers about his dream. He refused to go with them, and they returned to the land of Moab empty-handed.

'I will send even more noble messengers to Balaam,' Balak thought. 'I will heap gifts of silver and gold upon him, and then he will bring destruction down on the Israelites.'

Wasting no time, the king of Moab sent more messengers to Balaam – even more noble folk than before. They brought splendid gifts, and begged him to return with them to their kingdom and do as Balak asked.

Once again, however, Balaam would not give them an answer at once.

'God will tell me what to do,' he said. 'Stay the night in my house. In the morning I will give you my answer.'

Balaam did not sleep well that night. He would dearly have liked to do what Balak was asking. He longed to be welcomed with great ceremony, and could think of little else but his rich reward. God read his thoughts. He saw that Balaam set more store by the honour granted to him by worldly lords than by the will of the Lord of all things, so He allowed him to go as he wished. As soon as Balaam had set out to see the ruler of Moab, God showed him His power.

Balaam was riding an ass, and his two servants were with him. God caused an

angel with a drawn sword to appear before the ass, and seeing the messenger, the ass turned aside out of the way and went into the field. Balaam began to beat the ass to make it go the right way. Then the messenger of God went to stand on a vineyard path, bordered on either side by a wall. When the ass saw the angel, it pressed up against the wall, crushing Balaam's foot against it, and again he beat her. They then went on their way, but God's messenger again stepped in front of the ass, and this time the animal fell down under Balaam, who again beat it with his staff.

At that moment God gave the ass the gift of speech. 'Why are you beating me?' it asked. 'Have I not served you well?'

Balaam was amazed to hear an ass speak. At that moment God removed the veil from Balaam's eyes, and he saw the messenger of the Lord standing in the middle of the path.

'Why did you beat the donkey?' the angel asked. 'If it had not stepped aside, I should have killed you. You are the one who is guilty, for you have set out on an evil journey.'

Balaam flung himself face down on the ground. 'I have sinned against the Lord!' he cried. 'If God so wishes, I will go home, and will not go to Balak.'

'Continue on your way,' the messenger said. 'But you will say no more than what God puts on your lips.'

Balak welcomed Balaam joyfully. He had a sacrificial altar built, and sent for seven bulls and seven rams, as Balaam asked.

'Sacrifice the animals,' Balaam said to Balak. 'I will go up on to the high ground so as to see where the Israelites are camping on your borders. Perhaps God will meet me; if so, I will tell you what He says.'

When Balaam was standing in the appointed place, God did indeed speak to him. Balaam went back to Balak and said to him, 'Listen to me. God has said He does not curse the Israelites. How then can I? God has said He will not destroy them. How then can I? I wish I could be one of them!'

Enraged, Balak turned on Balaam, 'What have you done?' he cried out. 'You were to destroy my enemies, and now you have given them your blessing!'

'I am doing as God asked,' Balaam retorted.

Balak, filled with rage, would listen to Balaam no longer. He took Balaam to another high place from where the Israelites' camp could be seen, and said to him scornfully, 'Try to curse them from here.'

Balak prepared a sacrifice, and God spoke to Balaam again.

'What did you hear?' Balak wanted to know.

'God is not a man, who changes his decisions,' Balaam replied. 'I am to bless the people, and I cannot go against the word of God. My magic has no effect on the Israelites. God is with them, and they will defeat all those who wish to bring them to grief.'

'If you cannot destroy the Israelites, then at least do not bless them!' cried Balak. 'Come with me – I know another place. Perhaps God will let you curse them from there.'

Balak had a new altar constructed, and he sacrificed the best bulls and rams on it. He hoped in this way to find favour with God, but it was all in vain. Now Balaam himself had decided to bless God's people. From the top of the holy hill he looked down on the Israelites, camped around the tabernacle of God, and he called out, 'How splendid are your tents, O Israel! Thou shalt destroy thine enemies, and grind up their bones. Whoever blesses you will be blessed, and whoever curses you will be cursed himself!'

Balak turned upon Balaam in anger. 'Again you have blessed my enemies!' he shouted. 'Go back to where you came from! I wanted to give you a great reward, but God has taken it away from you.'

'I will go,' Balaam replied. 'But first you must listen to what will happen. My eyes see far into the distance; a new star is rising, the star of Israel. God's people will rule over you, and the chosen people of the Lord will take hold of your royal sceptre.'

With these words Balaam turned around, and left the land of Moab for ever. Before long these things happened as he had predicted. The Israelites defeated the Moab army. Balak, who wanted to conquer Israel, was himself humiliated. God had not abandoned His people. The way to the Promised Land was open.

Balaam Blesses Israel

The Promised Land

Moses had spent forty years in the desert, and was now very old. He felt that death was near, so he called Joshua, son of Nun, whom God had marked out to be his successor.

'Be resolute and bold,' Moses told Joshua before a gathering of all the Israelites. 'The time is at hand for you to take our people into the land which God promised our forefathers. Do not be afraid. The Lord will be with you, and will never abandon you.'

Joshua and the Israelites knew they would not see Moses again. They stood at the foot of Mount Nebo, on the borders of the Promised Land, and Moses spoke to them for the last time. He told them to keep God's commandments, and reminded them once again of God's words and deeds. The Israelites went to Moses, and he blessed them. Then he left the camp.

God told Moses to climb up Mountain Nebo towards Him, and Moses set off in the direction of His voice. At the summit he stopped. Far away in front of him he could see the land of Canaan, a land flowing with milk and honey. Moses was dying, but before he closed his eyes for the last time, he saw all the regions of that land. He saw the waves of the sea as they washed against the shore, and he saw the desert; he looked upon palm trees and deep valleys.

With his eyes fixed on the Promised Land, Moses died. He was buried in a valley in the land of Moab, near Bethpeor, and God took his soul into Heaven. The Israelites wept for Moses for thirty days, and then their mourning was over.

After the death of Moses, Joshua sent two scouts into the land of Canaan. They crossed the River Jordan and soon arrived in the city of Jericho. The scouts thought that no one had seen them, but the men of Jericho had noticed their coming. They saw them asking for shelter in one of the houses, and lost no time in telling their king.

The house belonged to a woman called Rahab. Early in the morning, when the scouts were still asleep, envoys from the king came pounding on her door.

'Give up the men who came here last night,' they ordered. 'They are spies of the Israelites.'

'They have already gone,' lied Rahab. 'I did not know who they were, so I let them go. If you set off after them at once, you will catch up with them.'

The king's messengers ran off into the city. The moment they had gone, she woke up the men and hid them on the roof of her house.

'I have heard of the power of your God,' she told them, 'and I know that the Lord has given you this land. All men quake with fear before you, so you must promise me that when you conquer the city of Jericho you will show mercy to me and to my family. Have I not saved your lives?'

'We will do as you ask,' the men told her, 'but you must not betray us, or tell anyone of our agreement. When we attack Jericho, get together in your house your father, mother and brothers. As soon as they are inside, hang the same scarlet cord by which we climbed from your house, in your window. That shall be a sign for us to spare your house.'

Rahab gave her word, and let them down out of her window by a cord, for her house was built into the town wall. Then she told them to run to the mountain where they could hide from their pursuers.

They ran there and waited in the mountain for three days. The royal soldiers searched for them in vain. They searched in the city and all around it, but they did not find the scouts.

Meanwhile the men returned to Joshua's camp and went to their leader. 'The Lord has delivered the whole of this land into our hands,' they said. 'All its inhabitants are shaking with fear before us.'

Before long the Israelites had set out in the direction of Jericho. On the banks of the River Jordan they stopped. The river was in flood, and the fields and paths were under water. One day passed, then two, then three, but the waters did not subside. The Israelites looked on helplessly, not knowing how to get across. Then God spoke to Joshua. 'Tomorrow I will work this miracle,' He said. 'Tell the priests who carry the Ark of the Covenant to stand beside the waters of the Jordan. They are to wet their feet, and to remain standing there.'

Joshua gave orders, and the priests did as the Lord had asked. As soon as the Ark of the Covenant was above the waters of Jordan, a wonderful thing happened. The running waters stopped, as if there were an invisible wall in front of them; then they built up, and formed a wall themselves. The water below this wall ran away, and dry land appeared beneath it. Now there was nothing to prevent the Israelites from crossing. The priests with the Ark of the Covenant stood where they were, and all the people went to the other bank and their feet remained dry.

'Now you see that the Lord is among you,' called Joshua. 'He will grant us victory over our enemies, and punish them for their evil. You will overrun their country, and live there according to the law of God.'

The last to cross the Jordan were the priests. The moment they stepped out of the river bed, the water began to flow once again. The wall of water came crashing down, and the river poured out over its banks again.

When the kings on the other side of the Jordan heard what God had done, they were filled with fear greater than ever. They shut themselves behind the walls of their cities, but neither their soldiers' weapons nor the thick walls could take away their fear.

Soon the Israelites were standing in front of the walls of Jericho. Joshua was preparing for battle, when he came across a stranger with a drawn sword.

'Are you one of us, or do you belong to the enemy?' asked Joshua.

'I am the captain of the heavenly army,' said the stranger who was an angel.

Joshua fell on his face to the ground, and said, 'What do you want me to do?'

The angel said, 'Take off your shoes, for you are on holy ground.'

Then God spoke to Joshua, saying, 'This is the way you will fight. Let seven priests with rams' horns walk around the city, and let the priests carrying the Ark of the Covenant walk behind them. In front of them shall be the soldiers, and behind them the rest of the people. Every day they must walk round Jericho once. On the seventh day they are to walk round the walls seven times. The priests will then blow a long blast on the horns, and the people will shout a great shout. The walls of the city will fall to the ground and you will have victory.'

Joshua assembled his army as God had told him. In front went the files of soldiers, behind them the priests with the horns. Next came the priests carrying the Ark and last were the old men, women and children.

The people of Jericho looked on in amazement at what the Israelites were do-

ing. They thought Joshua would attack at once, but instead the Israelites were walking around the walls. The people in the city did not know what to make of this, and many of them began to believe that the Israelites were afraid of the huge walls and the armed defenders. This went on for six days. On the seventh day the strange procession set out once again on its journey round the walls. This time, however, the Israelites walked around the city not once, but seven times. On the last trip the priests blew mightily on their horns. There was a long, fearful noise, mingling with the war-cries of the Israelites.

The walls of Jericho began to shake. Great stones fell away and the walls of Jericho crashed to the ground.

'Take the city!' cried Joshua to his

soldiers. The Lord has given us victory.'

The Israelites rushed into the streets, and all the inhabitants of Jericho and all their animals were destroyed.

Only Rahab's house was not touched. Rahab did not forget the sign she had a-greed, and she hung the scarlet cord in her window. When the Israelites saw it they led Rahab, her father, her mother and her brothers out of the city and had all their belongings taken to them. This was Rahab's reward for having concealed Joshua's spies.

Like Jericho, other cities fell to the Is-raelites. They conquered seven kingdoms, and made the whole of the Promised Land their own. The long and arduous journey of the Israelites was over. God had led His people to their own land.

Samson the Strong

While Joshua was still alive, the Israelites fared well. Each of them received his own portion of the Promised Land and were prosperous. After many years Joshua died, and they were led by others who ruled by the word of God. Before long the people turned away from their Creator. They began to live according to the customs of the surrounding peoples, and they broke God's wise laws and commandments.

God saw the evil which had spread among the Israelites, and grew angry with them. He left them at the mercy of the Philistines, who invaded a large part of the Promised Land. There were, though, many Israelites who were sorry for the sins they had committed, and so God decided that He would lessen the hardship of His people. His messenger visited an Israelite woman and said to her, 'You will soon become pregnant, and will give birth to a son who will avenge Israel. Do not drink wine or any other strong drink. Do not eat anything God has declared unclean. When the boy is born, do not cut his hair. That is the way God's chosen one is to live.'

The woman did not have any children, for she was unable, so the words of God's messenger surprised her. She ran to her husband, Manoah, and told him everything.

'Lord,' Manoah prayed to God, 'let your messenger come to us again, so that I, too, may hear how we are to look after our son.'

God answered Manoah's prayer. While his wife was working in the fields, God's messenger came to her again. She quickly called her husband. Manoah was told what was going to happen, and, overjoyed at the news, he wished to entertain his rare guest.

'Stay with us,' he entreated the angel. 'We will roast a kid for you.'

'There is no need,' the messenger told him. 'I would not eat your food. If you wish, you may sacrifice the kid to God.'

'What is your name?' Manoah asked the stranger.

'Do not ask,' the messenger replied. 'My name is secret.'

Manoah did not ask any more questions. He brought the kid and sacrificed it, but the moment the fire was lit, the Lord's messenger entered the flames and rose up among them to Heaven. Manoah and his wife hid their faces. 'We are sure to die,' said Manoah. 'We have seen God.'

Manoah's wife understood God's sign better than he did. 'If the Lord wanted to kill us,' she said, 'He would not accept our sacrifice, or tell us what the future holds. Do not be afraid.'

Then Manoah's wife did everything just as the messenger had stated, and she soon knew she was to have a child. When the time came she gave birth to a son whom she called Samson. From the day he was born until he grew up his hair was not cut. Samson was God's chosen one.

When he grew up, he told his mother and father, 'In Timnah I fell in love with a Philistine girl. I want to marry her.'

Samson's father and mother tried to change his mind. 'It would be better to marry one of our own girls,' they told him. 'Why have you chosen a bride from among our enemies?'

Samson would not listen to their words, and neither Manoah nor his wife tried to

stop him any longer. They did not know that it was God Himself who had led Samson to the woman, in order to show the Philistines that Israel would not remain conquered for ever.

On the way to Timnah, when Samson passed the vineyard, a young lion leaped upon him. He would have been killed, but God gave him strength, and Samson tore the lion apart with his bare hands. He told no one about what had happened. In Timnah he arranged to be married, and went home again.

After several days Samson set off back for Timnah to get married. When he reached the spot where he had killed the lion, he saw that some bees were nesting in the carcase. He ate some of their honey, and before long he was sitting at the wedding feast. In the midst of the celebrations he turned round to the thirty Philistine youths who had come to join them.

'I wish to set you a riddle,' he told them. 'If you can guess it within a week, I will give you thirty sheets and thirty changes of clothes. If you do not guess it, I will get the same gift from you.'

The Philistines agreed, and Samson said, 'Here is my riddle. Out of the eater came food, and out of the strong came sweetness.'

The Philistine youths thought for three days, and could not guess the answer, but since they did not want to miss out on their rich reward, they said to Samson's wife, 'Get your husband to tell you the answer.

Samson the Strong

If you do not, we will burn you and your father's house.'

So Samson's wife began to ask questions. She begged him, saying, 'You cannot love me if you will not tell me the answer,' and she wept until he told her what she needed to know. Then she told the Philistine youths, and they came to Samson.

'We know the answer to your question,' they said proudly. 'What is sweeter than honey, or stronger than a lion?'

Samson knew that his wife had betrayed him. In a great rage he went off and killed thirty Philistines in a nearby city. He tore their clothes off them and gave them to the thirty youths he had promised to reward. Then he returned to his father's house, staying there for some time.

When the time came to reap wheat, Samson wanted to go and see what his wife was doing, but her father would not let him into the house. 'You left in anger, and so I have given your wife to another,' he told Samson. 'If you wish, you may marry her younger sister.'

Samson grew fearfully angry. He caught three hundred foxes, tied them in twos by their tails and fixed burning torches to them. Then he sent them into the Philistines' grainfields, and their corn, vines and olives were burned down.

When the Philistines heard about this they were filled with hatred. In vengeance they killed Samson's wife and her father, and then set out with an army against the Israelites.

The Israelites were very much afraid. They asked the Philistines why they were going to war, and they were told of Samson's deeds.

'What have you done?' the people demanded of Samson. 'Do you not know that the Philistines are our masters? We will bind you and deliver you to them, rather than suffer for what you have done.'

'Do that,' replied Samson. 'But do not kill me.'

The Israelites promised to spare his life. They bound him with strong ropes and led him into the Philistines' camp.

The Philistines let out a joyous cry, but then God gave Samson strength. He broke free from the ropes as though they had been made of sewing thread. Then he picked up the jawbone of an ass that was lying by the wayside, and fought with it as if it

were a sword. With it he killed a thousand Philistines, and the rest took flight.

From then on the Philistines stayed away from Samson. They knew that God gave him strength, and that they could not defeat him in battle. So they decided to overcome him by a trick. They followed him around, trying to find out the secret of his strength.

Soon the Philistines found out that Samson was in love with a girl named Delilah. They sent their noblemen to her with promises of much silver if she told them how to overcome Samson.

Delilah waited impatiently for Samson to come. As soon as he appeared, she began to implore him, 'Tell me, why are you so strong? What ropes must be used to tie

Samson the Strong

you up so that you cannot break them?'

'If my enemies were to bind me with seven green switches, I should be as helpless as any other men,' he told her.

So the Philistines brought seven green switches to Delilah, and she bound him in his sleep. The Philistines were waiting in his bedchamber and they hurled themselves upon Samson bent on killing him. Instead, he woke up, tore off his bonds, and killed them all.

Then Delilah again asked Samson what he might be tied with that he could not break.

Samson loved Delilah, so he told her, 'I would not be able to break new ropes that had never been used.'

So Delilah bound Samson with new ropes, and called the Philistines. Yet as soon as they attacked him he broke out of his bonds again, and again they did not destroy him.

'You have deceived me a second time,' said Delilah, angrily. 'Why do you not want to tell me where your strength comes from?'

'If you were to plait seven locks of my hair into a warp, I should not be able to defend myself,' Samson told her.

So Delilah did as Samson had said. She called the Philistines, but as soon as they came near to Samson he woke up. With one heave he broke his bonds and killed the Philistines.

'Why do you make fun of me?' Delilah asked him crossly. 'You have lied to me three times; you do not love me at all! If

you were to think of me, you would tell me the truth!'

Delilah beseeched Samson day and night, until in the end he gave way. 'My hair has never been cut,' he told her, 'which is why I have been dedicated to God since I was born. If my hair were to be cut, I should be like any other man.'

Delilah saw that Samson was telling the truth this time. 'Come once more,' was the message she sent to the Philistine noblemen. 'I know the secret of Samson's strength.'

Silently, the Philistines gathered in the house. First of all Delilah put Samson to sleep, then she called one of the men to shave his head and bind him.

'The Philistines are upon you, Samson!' Delilah cried.

Samson leapt from his bed. He tried to

Samson the Strong

break his bonds as before, but he had lost all his strength along with his hair. The Philistines threw themselves upon him. They blinded him, and bound him in brass shackles, then threw him into prison.

To celebrate this victory, the Philistines held a great celebration in the noblemen's palace. 'Our god Dagon has saved us,' they cried. 'We have overcome Samson; the God of Israel did not help him.'

The feasting lasted for many days and nights. When the Philistines grew merry, they began to call out, 'Bring Samson here, we will have some fun with him. We will make fun of him and laugh at his strength.'

The guards led Samson out of his prison and placed him between the columns which held up the palace of the Philistine nobles. No one thought anything of the fact that his hair had grown again. Blind and unarmed, the Philistines laughed at him.

'Let me feel the columns,' Samson asked the man who led him in.

The Philistine did not suspect anything, so he held Samson's hands up against the cold stone. At that instant Samson called out, 'Lord, Master, remember me, and give me the last strength to avenge Israel and my own eyes!'

With these words Samson leaned against the pillars of the palace and cried once more, 'Let me die along with the Philistines!'

The pillars came crashing down, and the palace, with nothing to hold it up was flat-

tened, killing all the Philistine noblemen and thousands of soldiers. Samson died with them. His brothers dug his body out of the ruins and with sadness in their hearts, buried it.

There had never been such a man as Samson. He left behind strength and hope for his people.

Samson the Strong

Naomi and Ruth

A t the time when the land of Israel did not yet have a king, it was ruled over by judges, men of great truth and justice, who were close to God. A great famine arrived. The grain would not grow in the fields, and the fruit on the trees withered before it ripened. Neither men nor animals had enough to eat. In those evil days there was in Bethlehem a man named Elimelech and his wife Naomi. They had sons called Mahlon and Chilion. In their house, too, there was barely any food. Elimelech's neighbours were in similar straits, but he was the only one who thought it would be wise to leave Israel and go elsewhere in search of food. So he sold some of his belongings, and, taking his wife and sons with him, set out for the land of Moab.

God, however, was not pleased with Elimelech's journey. Before he had been in Moab very long, Elimelech fell ill and died. Naomi was left on her own with her sons. After a while, Chilion and Mahlon married Moab women, and Naomi hoped her grandchildren would know times of plenty. Ten years passed and Naomi met with even greater misfortune. Mahlon and Chilion both died, leaving their wives alone to look after their children.

When Naomi had buried her sons, she called in her daughters-in-law and said to them, 'I have heard that God has been good to my people. There is food again in the land of Israel, and so I will return home. You should stay here and find husbands among your own people and be happy.'

Both the girls burst into tears. They loved Naomi and did not want her to go. So they said, 'We do not want you to leave. Surely you would let us go with you?'

'Why do you want go with me?' asked Naomi. 'It would be better if you were to stay here. There is a strict law in my country: if a woman has no children and her husband dies, she must marry his brother or another of his relatives. She then gives him children, so that the family does not die out. But I am old. I have no sons, and I do not know if any of my relations are alive. I do not want you to be left without husbands.'

At this the girls wept even more loudly. The first of them, Orpah, kissed her mother-in-law and took leave of her, but the other, who was called Ruth, did not want to leave Naomi.

'Do not go with me,' Naomi tried to per-

119

suade her. 'Go back to your people like Orpah.'

Then Ruth replied, 'Wherever you go, I will go too. Wherever you remain, I will stay too. Your people will be my people, and your God my God. Let the Lord do with me what He will. Only death shall part us.'

When Naomi saw that Ruth was determined to follow her, she did not try to change her mind. They set off together for the land of Israel, and arrived together in Bethlehem, where Naomi had lived many years before. It was summer, and the barley harvest was beginning. Naomi had no money to buy food, and her husband's fields had not been tilled. So Ruth said, 'I will go and gather the ears the reapers have left behind on the edge of the field. Maybe God will lead me to the field of someone who will be kind to me.'

Not far from Bethlehem the breeze rippled a huge field of grain. As luck would have it, Ruth had found the field of Boaz straight away. She entered the field, and walking behind the reapers, began to pick up the ears of corn they had left behind.

While Ruth was in the field, Boaz came from Bethlehem to see how the harvest was getting on. As he stood talking to his head man, he asked, 'Who is the girl in the field?'

'Ruth of the Moabians,' replied the man who was watching over the reapers' work.

Then Boaz went to Ruth, and seeing him coming, she became frightened. She need not have worried, for Boaz spoke to her kindly.

'Do not gather the fallen ears in any other field,' he told her. 'Do not leave this place. I have ordered my servants not to trouble you or drive you away. If you are thirsty, go to them and they will give you water from their vessels.'

Ruth bowed to Boaz and said, 'Why are you kind to me, when I am a foreigner?'

'Do not be surprised,' Boaz replied. 'I know how kind you were to Naomi when her husband and sons died. You left your own mother and father, you left your own people to live with one that was strange to you. May the God of Israel be merciful to you and reward you for your good heart.'

That day Ruth gathered a large number of ears. Boaz ordered his reapers to drop them on purpose, and when the time came to eat he offered her bread to eat. She ate her fill and had some left over. Then she

flailed the ears she had gathered and went
back to Naomi.

'Where were you working?' Naomi
asked.

'In Boaz's field,' was the reply. 'He was
kind and generous to me.'

Naomi was pleased. 'God has been good
to us,' she said. 'Boaz is a relative of my
husband, a wise and respected man. He is
not yet married, therefore you may be
thankful that it was him who stood up for
you. I am sure he could not help but like
you.'

The next day Ruth went to Boaz's field
again and walked along it until the barley
had been reapcd. What she gathered during the day she flailed in the early evening,

and took the grain to her mother-in-law. Boaz was kinder to Ruth day by day. He saw how faithfully she served Naomi, and he liked her hard working ways and kind heart. Ruth also liked to see Boaz, but she did not dare show her affection for him, so Naomi told her, 'Tonight Boaz will sleep in the courtyard. When he is asleep, uncover his feet and lie down by them. If you do as tell you, you will fare well.'

The moment darkness fell on Bethlehem, Ruth went into Boaz's courtyard. She crept up to Boaz, who was sleeping on a pile of grain, uncovered his feet and snuggled up against them. At midnight Boaz woke up. He looked around and suddenly saw the sleeping woman close by. At first he was startled, but when he saw that it was Ruth, he smiled. 'It is good that you came,' he said. 'You have proved how faithful you are to me, and I know that you enjoy God's favour. He has protected you with His strength, and I too want to protect you. I am a relation of your dead husband, and according to the law of Israel I want to marry you. There is, however, another man in Bethlehem who is more closely related to your dead husband than I am. He must have first choice. In case he does not want you, you shall become my wife.'

Then Boaz gave Ruth a great deal of grain, and sent her home to Naomi.

Ruth came home confused and frightened. She loved Boaz, not some stranger, and was afraid the other man would not refuse her. Naomi then said to her, 'Do not be afraid. Everything is going well. You will become Boaz's wife this very day.'

While the two of them were speaking in this way, Boaz sat beside the city gate and waited for the man he had told Ruth about. Before long he saw him coming. Boaz called ten of the city elders as witnesses and said, 'Naomi who has returned from the land of Moab, wishes to sell her dead husband's Elimelech's fields.

You are his closest relative, and so you have preference.'

The man did not hesitate for long. 'I will buy them,' he said.

'But in that case you must marry Ruth, who came with Naomi,' Boaz told him. 'She is the widow of Elimelech and Naomi, and the fields belong to her, too. If you buy the fields, you are obliged to preserve the family of the dead father and son.'

The man had not expected this. Having other plans, he turned down Boaz's offer.

'Ten witnesses have heard your reply,' Boaz said triumphantly. 'If you do not want to buy Naomi's fields, I do. They belong to me and according to the law of our land so does Ruth, the woman the Lord had blessed.'

The elders of the city confirmed the bargain, and so a wedding took place. None of the guests was more joyful than Naomi. Her years of sadness had ended, and she enjoyed the favour of the Lord once more. When Ruth gave birth to a son, Obed, Naomi was his nurse. From this house, many years later came none other than David, King of Israel.

Naomi and Ruth

Samuel – Judge of Israel

During the time when the priest Eli was judge in Israel, a certain man lived in the town of Ramah whose name was Elkanah. In the ancient days it was the custom to have several wives, and Elkanah had two. The first of them, Peninnah, gave birth to many sons and daughters, but the second, Hannah, was childless. Elkanah loved Hannah with all his heart, and he tried to comfort her in this misfortune.

'Why are you weeping?' he always asked her when she was sad. 'Am I not more to you than ten sons?'

Yet however kind he was towards Hannah, he could not take away her sadness. The more fortunate of his wives, Peninnah, was always laughing at Hannah because she had no children, until Hannah was so sad she could not even eat.

Every year, on the day of the feast of God, Elkanah and his family used to travel to Shiloh, where the Lord's temple stood, with the Ark of the Covenant and the Ten Commandments. There they would pray to the Lord. One year Hannah took her leave of the others, and went to one side to speak to the Lord. 'O God,' she prayed tearfully, 'take pity on me in my sadness, and remember me. Give me a baby boy, and I will dedicate him to you. He shall be your chosen one, if only you grant my prayer.'

The priest Eli stood by the door of the temple and watched Hannah praying. Her lips moved, but her voice could not be heard.

'She is drunk,' Eli thought. 'Put away your wine!' he shouted angrily.

'I am not drunk,' Hannah replied. 'I am only sad. I am calling upon God in my desperation and grief, so do not think ill of me.'

Eli realized then that she was speaking the truth. 'May the God of Israel grant your wish,' he told her. 'Go in peace.'

Not long after Eli had given her his blessing, Hannah found she was going to have a baby. Before the year was out she had given birth to a son, whom she called Samuel, meaning *God granted*. That year Hannah did not make the pilgrimage to Shiloh.

'When the boy has been weaned, I will take him to the holy place to serve God forever,' she told her husband. 'I have dedicated Samuel to the Lord, and I will keep my promise.'

The days went by, and the boy grew a little. The time came for Hannah to take him to Shiloh. She loaded many gifts on to a cart, and then went in search of Eli the priest. When she found him, she said, 'I am the woman who prayed to the Lord before your eyes. I prayed the Lord to give me a boy, and He had granted my wishes. Now I am bringing the boy to you, as I have dedicated him to God. He will belong to Him as long as he will live.'

So Samuel lived with Eli the priest in Shiloh. Eli watched over him, and Samuel served in the Lord's shrine.

The priest Eli had two sons, Hophni and Phinehas, who would one day take on the high priest's robes. But they were evil and godless, wicked in word and in deed. They ignored the ways of the Lord when it came to sacrifice, and would, when someone

Samuel – Judge of Israel

brought an animal to be sacrificed, take the meat which should have been burned in honour of God, and roast it to eat. If anyone tried to stop them they took the meat by force. They abused their priestly office and the name of God.

The sins of Hophni and Phinehas were great indeed, for they led people astray from the Creator. Hannah and Elkanah visited their son every time they went to Shiloh. Each time Hannah brought him a new robe and Eli blessed her and Elkanah.

Many years passed by. Hannah gave

birth to three more sons and two daughters. Samuel grew up and Eli grew old. He heard about the misdeeds of his sons, and was saddened by them. 'You encourage the people of God to break his laws,' he told them. 'Why do you commit such a sin? If man sins against man, God can forgive him, but who is to forgive you, if you sin against God Himself?'

He often found fault with them like this, but he always forgave them. So Hophni and Phinehas took no notice of him. They saw that their father loved them with a blind love, and carried on in their evil ways.

Then the God's messenger came to Eli and said, 'This is the word of the Lord. Your family was chosen from among the others to be a family of priests. Hophni and Phinehas ride roughshod over my laws, and do not respect my sacrifices. Since you honour your sons more than you honour me, Eli, listen to what I say. Those who honour me will be rewarded, whereas those who disdain me can expect punishment. Your sons will soon die; they will not serve in my temple. I will choose my own priest.'

Not long after that, in the middle of the night, Eli was resting in the Lord's temple. He was old now, and his sight was failing. Samuel, too, was in the house of the Lord. God spoke to him.

'I am here,' said Samuel.

He thought it was Eli calling him, and he went over to the priest, but Eli said, 'I did not call you. Go back.'

Samuel did as he was told, but as soon as he went away from Eli, he heard again a voice calling his name. He ran to Eli again, to ask why he had called him.

'I did not speak to you either the first time or this time,' said the priest. 'Go to your place.'

God does not often speak to people in this way, and Samuel did not know that it was the Creator himself who was talking to him. Eli realized however, and when Samuel came a third time Eli told him, 'If the voice speaks to you again, you should answer, "Speak, Lord, your servant can hear you."'

The moment Samuel was alone, God

Samuel – Judge of Israel

called out his name. Samuel replied as Eli had told him, and God said, 'I have passed judgement on Eli and all his house, because he did not condemn the crimes of Hophni and Phinehas, but to you, Samuel, I will give my spirit. You shall become my prophet, and what you say will happen. You will be a judge in Israel, and shall lead the unbelievers to the way of truth.'

Samuel bowed down to God, and stayed there until the Sun rose. In the morning Eli called to him, 'Samuel, my son,' he said.

'What did the Lord speak to you about? Do not hide anything from me.'

Samuel was afraid to tell his teacher what he had heard, but in the end he gave away God's secret.

Eli bowed his head. 'Let God do what is right,' he whispered. 'Only he can judge.'

It was not long before God's judgement was carried out. Eli and his sons all died on the same day. Samuel took Eli's place as priest and remained so until the end of his days.

Samuel – Judge of Israel

David – God's Anointed

I n the days when the wise Samuel was judge in Israel, God's people again heard the word of their maker. The Israelites obeyed His Commandments, and God took their part. With His help they drove the Philistines out of their land. Then they made a treaty of peace with all their neighbours, and peace reigned.

When Samuel grew old, the elders of the people went to him and said, 'We do not want your sons to rule after your death. Give us a king, so that we may have a noble ruler like the other nations.'

Samuel warned the Israelites that there was no greater ruler than the Lord, that human kings were weak, but they would not listen. The Israelites longed to have a king of their own, so God heard their prayers. He gave them a new ruler, a tall

and handsome man. His name was Saul. When he began to rule, Samuel was still alive. He called Saul to him and said, 'Hear the word of God. The time of peace has come to an end. You will soon be at war with the Philistines, and when they attack, I will not be here, but will serve God in another place. After seven days I will come into your camp. Wait for me and do nothing. I will tell you what you are to do.'

It happened in the second year of Saul's reign, just as Samuel had foretold. The armies of the Israelites and the Philistines

went to battle. The Philistines had gathered together a thousand of war chariots and six thousand riders, and there were as many foot soldiers as there are grains of sand on the seashore.

When the Israelites saw to them what seemed like a human flood, they were no longer brave. Some of them ran away to hide in caves and among the rocks, while others fled to high places or hid in pits. Saul himself was afraid. Anxiously he waited for Samuel, but the judge of Israel was nowhere to be seen. Meanwhile, Saul's frightened people were deserting him. His army grew smaller every day, and there was still no sign of Samuel. On the seventh day Saul could not bear it any

longer. 'Who knows when Samuel will come,' he thought. 'I shall just have to manage on my own. I will make a sacrifice to the Lord, so that he answers my prayers.'

So Saul made a sacrifice, but the moment the smoke of his fire began to rise towards heaven, Samuel appeared beside him. 'What have you done?' he cried. 'Did I not tell you to wait for me? God Himself spoke through my mouth, and you did not believe Him. If you had obeyed His command, He would have made you king forever, but since you have scorned the words of the Lord, you will not rule much longer. God will seek out another man, and make him king of the Israelites.'

So God soon turned His face away from

Saul. The Philistines went on tormenting the Israelites, and the land was in great danger. The just judge Samuel was very worried about this. One day, when he was feeling very disheartened, God spoke to him again. 'Go to a man called Jesse in the city of Bethlehem,' he told him. 'I have found myself a king among his sons.'

Samuel did as the Lord had told him. He took the horn of holy oil to anoint God's chosen one, and set out for Bethlehem. The first person he saw in Jesse's house was his eldest son, Eliab, a tall and strongly built young man. 'This will surely be the next king of Israel,' Samuel thought.

Then he heard the word of God. 'You are wrong, Samuel. Your eyes see only the face and body, but I can see into the human heart. Go on looking.'

Then Jesse's second son, Abinadab, came before Samuel.

'No,' God said. 'He is not chosen, either.'

One after another, seven of Jesse's sons came before Samuel, but not one of them was worthy to become king of Israel. Samuel trusted in the word of God, so he asked Jesse, 'Have you any more sons?'

'Only the youngest, David,' Jesse replied, 'but he is not at home. He is a herdsman, and he is out in the pastures with the sheep.' 'Send for him at once,' Samuel told him. 'Quickly!'

It was not long before the messengers brought Jesse's son. He was red-haired, with beautiful eyes, a small man, but strong.

'He is the one, my chosen one,' God said to Samuel. 'Anoint him king of Israel.'

Samuel poured the holy oil on David's head. Neither David nor his brothers understood what this meant. In their eyes the king was Saul, but Saul was no longer king in the eyes of God.

Not long after that the Philistines attacked again. They camped on a mountain, and the Israelites occupied the opposite hill, with a valley in between. There was one very strong, very tall warrior among the Philistines, and his name was Goliath. He towered above the other soldiers, and it took several men to carry his weapons. In his coat of mail, with his brass helmet on his head and guards on his legs, he would go every morning and evening to the valley, wave his bronze sword above his head, and call out to the Israelites, 'Send me a man who is not afraid. Let him try his strength against mine. If he kills me in battle, the Philistines will become your slaves, but if I am victorious, you shall serve us.'

The Israelites shook with fear at the sight of Goliath. No one dared challenge him to a combat, and the Philistines were pleased at the fear of the Israelites.

David's three eldest brothers, Eliab, Abinadab and Shammah, were in the Israelite army. One day their father called David and said, 'Go into the camp to take bread and roast grain to your brothers.'

David left the flocks in the care of his companion and went to do as his father asked him. He reached the place where his

brothers were camped, just in time to see Goliath come out and boast about his strength. He mocked the Israelites, and threatened them, and they ran back.

Then David heard one of the soldiers saying, 'Saul says that whoever kills Goliath will not lack either riches or honour.'

'I will go,' cried David, without hesitation. 'I want to fight Goliath!'

'What is this you are saying?' David's eldest brother demanded. 'You have only just left your flocks. This is too bold of you; you only came here to watch the fighting.'

Yet David insisted. Again and again he said that he would fight Goliath, until in the end Saul himself heard about it. He called David and said to him, 'I hear you want to fight Goliath. How can you succeed against him, when you are young and inexperienced, and he has been a warrior for many years?'

'A man should never despair,' David replied. 'If a lion or a bear came to carry off my sheep, I killed them with my own hands. God has always saved me from the claws of wild beasts and He will help me fight against Goliath.'

Saul saw that David was serious about his desire to fight Goliath and he did not try to stop him. He lent the boy his own armour, and placed the royal sword in his hand.

But David said, 'I am not used to fighting in armour. I should perfer my own clothes.'

He quickly took off the precious armour, and with an ordinary shepherd's staff in his hand he went out to face the terrible Goliath. The path led him alongside a stream. David bent down and picked up a few pebbles, and put them in his shepherd's bag, where he already had a strong sling.

When Goliath saw David, he began to

laugh. 'Am I a dog,' he mocked, 'that you bring a stick to hit me with? Come closer, so that I may throw your body to the birds and wild beasts!'

David was not afraid. 'You come to me with a sword, a lance and a spear,' he replied, 'but I come in the name of the Lord. You have shamed the Lord's people, and for that you must answer!'

Goliath came forward menacingly. Suddenly, David put his hand in his bag. Taking one of the stones he had just put in there, he swung his sling and sent it flying with full force. Goliath gave a cry as the stone struck him full on in the middle of his forehead. The Philistine staggered and fell to the ground. That was what David was waiting for. He leaped up to the stunned giant, drew his sword from its sheath, and with a single blow chopped off his head.

The Israelites gave a great cheer, and taking their weapons in hand, they rushed forward as one man. The Philistines took flight. Terrified by Goliath's death, they fled in all directions, anxious to save their lives at all costs.

In the meantime David returned in triumph to the Israelite camp. Laying Goliath's armour down in his tent, he carried the defeated Philistine's head before Saul. After that David remained at court. Saul made him his servant, but God had decided that the servant should become the master. Saul's days were numbered. The king of Israel, the Lord's anointed, was called David, son of Jesse of Bethlehem.

Saul's Plot

When God overthrew Saul, the unworthy king of Israel was possessed by an evil spirit. As soon as it took over, Saul raged like one insane, until all his subjects ran away from him in fear.

'Find yourself a servant who can play the zither,' they advised Saul in a moment of calm. 'The music will comfort your mind, and you will forget your pain and suffering.'

There was no better musician in the land of Israel than David. He was skilled with the sword, but his fingers also made the strings of the zither sing. David's wonderful melodies comforted better than any medicine, so he always came to Saul when he was feeling depressed.

The pleasant music brought Saul relief, but his soul could not find peace. He had noted how popular David was. He regretted that the people praised his victory over the terrible Goliath, and he envied him his hero's honour. 'They think more of David than of me,' he thought, bitterly. 'Before long he will be king in my place.'

That was indeed God's will, but Saul did not know that. He was more and more jealous of David, and hatred made him blind to God's plan.

One day Saul was again troubled by his illness. He called David to him and with a lance in his hand listened to his music. Suddenly, Saul raised his arm and threw the lance at David. David managed to avoid it, but Saul, like a man demented,

drew the weapon out of the wall and threw it again. Once more it whistled throught the air, and again David dodged it. He left unharmed, and Saul began to be afraid of him.

From that day on he could think of nothing else but how to rid himself of David.

'I will give you my daughter for your wife,' he told him, 'if you kill two hundred Philistines.'

Saul hoped that David would die before

he killed the first few warriors, but before long he had completed his task. Like it or not, Saul was obliged to keep his promise. David married Saul's daughter Michal, and Saul's hatred grew stronger than ever. The more unpleasant he became, the more the rest of the people loved David. Even Saul's son Jonathan grew to like David, and became his great friend and protector.

'Why should you spill innocent blood?' Jonathan asked his father. 'Did not David save us from Goliath? He delivered Israel, and he must not die just because of your blind hatred.'

Saul promised to spare David's life. 'When the evil spirit comes upon me,' he begged David, 'play your zither to relieve my troubles.'

It was not long before Saul again became wild, but as soon as David came to soothe his spirits, Saul threw his lance at him again. 'I will impale you to the wall!' he shouted crazily. 'You are going to die, David!'

That night God saved David. With the Lord's help he escaped from the palace and hid in his own house. Then Saul told his servants, 'Hide near to David's house, and when he comes out in the morning, kill him!'

David's wife Michal heard what was being planned. She quickly woke David up and while it was still dark let him out of a window into the garden. The soldiers waited for him but he did not come. When the Sun was high in the sky, they rushed into the house. Though they searched high and low, they found only Michal. David had escaped.

When Saul heard what had happened, he sent speedy messengers after David to capture him. They caught up with him in Naioth in Ramah, at the house of the prophet Samuel. 'We have come to arrest you!' they shouted.

At that moment they saw Samuel and the other priests, in a prophet's trance. The spirit of God came over the messengers also, and they prayed to God and forgot all about David.

So Saul sent more men after David. 'You must capture him,' he told them. 'I want David to die!'

These messengers arrived in Ramah, but they, too, were unable to carry out their orders. Before they were able to attack David, they saw what they were about to do and begged God's forgiveness. So Saul's plans had failed again.

Saul still would not accept that David was God's chosen one. He sent more men to Ramah, again ordering them to bring David to him. They rode away, but again did not return. After several days, Saul set off himself to find David. When he got to his house he found all his servants there. They were confessing to their sins and taking no notice of David. Suddenly, Saul was filled with the Lord's spirit. He fell to the ground in fear and awe, and remained there all night.

At dawn, when Saul and his men came out of their trance, David was gone. Saul still did not give up. He sent his servants out in all directions and soon found out where David was. Wherever he went, Saul followed him. He hunted David like a wild beast and he and his armed men pursued him from place to place. David was no longer alone, however. Along the way he was joined by people similar to himself, good men and good warriors, who made David their leader.

After a long journey, Saul and his armed men finally caught up with David and his

followers and surrounded them at a place near Keilah. Saul gathered together three thousand soldiers, and felt certain of victory.

'We will hide in the caves,' David decided, when he saw how heavily outnumbered they were. 'Perhaps Saul will not find us.'

God, who directs the steps of all living things, led Saul to the cave where David had taken refuge. It was midday, and the Sun blazed down from high in the sky. Saul went inside the cave to shelter from the heat. He had no idea that in the far corner, unseen to him, was David and his best warriors. 'You can do with Saul what you will,' David's men whispered to him. 'You only have to give the order, and we will kill him.'

Instead of replying, David crept up on Saul. After secretly cutting off the corner of Saul's cloak, he went back to his place. 'Let God decide Saul's fate,' he told his companions. 'I will not commit a crime. Saul is my master.'

Saul went out of the cave and continued on his way. When he had gone a short distance, David called out to him, 'Master!'

Saul turned round and saw David, who bowed low towards him.

'Why do you think I am trying to destroy you?' David called out. 'Look – I have in my hand the corner of your cloak. I could have killed you, and I chose, however, to spare you. Yet you are trying to kill me, although I have not harmed you.'

Saul began to weep. 'You are more just than I am,' he said to David. 'Who would let his enemy walk away, when he was at his mercy? Now I know that only you can be king of Israel. May the Lord reward you for your deed.'

Saul's words were not the same as his thoughts. While David had been away from home, he had given his wife Michal to a servant of his named Phalti. David repaid Saul's evil with good, but Saul returned evil for good. He forgot his blessing,

and again tried to take David's life. He followed him by night and day, until he caught up with him in the desert of Ziph.

Saul and his army pitched camp and prepared for battle. When darkness came, David asked his followers, 'Who will go with me to Saul's camp?'

'I will go with you,' said a young man named Abishai.

So they fastened their swords to their belts and set off. Slipping through the sentries unseen they reached Saul's tent, which was pitched in the middle of the

camp in a trench, surrounded by all the others. Saul was asleep on his bed. There was a jug of water by his head, and his lance was stuck in the ground. Next to him slept his general, Abner. Neither he nor his master had any idea who was bending over them.

'Give the order, and I will slay Saul with a single blow,' Abishai told David. 'God has placed him in your hands.'

'No, that is not God's wish,' David told him. 'As the Lord lives, so He will punish Saul, but I will not spill his blood. Take only his jug and his lance. I ask no more.'

David and his servant left as silently as they had come. No one woke up, for God had placed a deep sleep on everyone in the camp. At dawn David climbed a hill close to Saul's camp.

'Saul!' he called. 'Saul! Look at your lance and the water jug which stood beside your head. I could have killed you, but for a second time I spared your life. I let you live; now it is your turn to let me live. Why do you still want to kill me?'

Saul looked up to the top of the hill from where David's voice came. He recognized his lance and water jug, and was ashamed.

'You will surely do many great deeds, David,' he said. 'Go in peace.'

Only God sees into the hearts of men, only He knows when they speak the truth. Saul promised to leave David in peace many times, but he never kept his word. For this reason the wrath of God descended on him. All on the same day he and his three sons died, and David never again had need to fear him.

Saul's Plot

David's Sin

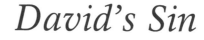

Davd was thirty years old when he became king of all Israel.

'You shall lead my people like a shepherd looking after his sheep,' God told him. 'Your house and your kingdom will carry on, and the throne which you reign will last for ever.'

God's blessing stayed with David for the rest of his life. He defeated the neighbouring tribes, which hated Israel, and stood on the holy mountains of his enemies and on the banks of great rivers. In times of peace he remained in the old city of Jerusalem, where he lived in a beautiful palace of cedar wood, and not far away, in the holy temple, was the Ark of the Covenant containing the tablets on which the Ten Commandments were written. Peace reigned over the whole of the kingdom of Israel.

David's Sin

God was good to David and David was good to his people.

Things stayed the same for many years. One day, when the army of the Israelites was setting out to do battle once more, David stayed behind in Jerusalem. He could rely on the fighting skills of his army, so he waited calmly for news from the battlefield. In the early evening he went out on to the flat roof of his palace and looked down on the city with satisfaction. He was looking at its white walls and narrow streets, when he suddenly saw, in the garden of a house not far away, the most beautiful woman he had ever seen.

'Who is she?' he asked the servants, and they answered at once, 'Bathsheba, wife of Uriah, who is fighting with the army.'

David wanted more than anything to be with Bathsheba. He paid no heed to the fact that she belonged to another man, and thought of nothing than how to win her. His great need to have her changed him, and he could think of nothing else.

'Bring Bathsheba to me!' he ordered his servants. 'Have her come before the king!'

Bathsheba could not refuse, and stayed with David until morning, as if she were his wife.

After several weeks Bathsheba sent a message to David, saying, 'I am going to have your child.'

It was only now that David realized how foolishly he had acted. 'It would be better if no one were to know of it,' he thought, and he tried to cover up his evil deed. 'Send me Bathsheba's husband Uriah from the camp,' he ordered. 'I must speak to him.'

David was not interested in confessing to Uriah. He only wanted Uriah to come home in order that he may spend some

thought about his next move, but the more he tried to cover up his evil doings, the more evil he committed. Before Uriah went back to the battlefield, David gave him a letter. 'Give this message to Joab, your general,' he told him. 'Do not forget!'

Uriah bowed to David, and before long Joab was holding the royal letter. 'Send Uriah to the place where the battle is fiercest,' it said. 'Then all the rest of you should retreat. I want Uriah to die in battle.'

At the time the army of Israel was besieging the city of Rabbah. There was one place which was defended by particularly good soldiers, and it was there that Joab sent Uriah. There was a cruel struggle. Uriah fought bravely, but suddenly he found himself alone. A hail of arrows fell upon him from the enemy ramparts, and Uriah died instantly.

When Uriah's wife heard the sad news, she wept for her dead husband for many days. Yet no grief lasts for ever. The period of mourning passed, and Bathsheba accepted David's invitation to become the wife of the king. Soon after they were married she gave birth to a son, the fruit of David's sin. No one knew about the child's real father. They thought he was Uriah's son. Everyone felt sorry for the boy, born after his father's death, and they praised the nobility of David, who had taken in the unhappy widow. David could not deceive God, however, for He knew the truth and was angry at the evil David had done.

time with his wife. 'Then, when the child was born,' thought David, 'everyone would think it was Uriah's child. It would bear Uriah's name, and people would say, "God has blessed him with offspring." They would congratulate Uriah and suspect no evil.'

Uriah was a man of honour, however. 'How can I sleep on a soft bed beside my wife, when my fellows are lying on the ground on the battlefield?' he asked. 'I will not enter my house.'

That night he lay down beside the entrance to the royal palace and did not go to his wife the next day either, or the next.

David's plan had failed. Desperate, he

David's Sin

In those days the prophet Nathan was passing through Israel. God led his steps and put His words in his mouth. He sent him to David to tell him:

'In a certain city there lived two men, one rich and one poor. The rich man had many cows, sheep and horses, whereas the poor man had only a single sheep, which he loved very dearly. He gave her his own bread, let her drink from his cup, and had her sleep on his lap. One day a guest came to the rich man's house. The rich man wanted to give him a good meal, but he was too mean to want to kill one of his own sheep, and he took the poor man's ewe, which he slew and served to his guest.'

David burst into a rage. 'The man who committed such a crime must die!' he cried. 'Since he treated the man so badly, he must return the poor man what he took fourfold!'

'What you say is right,' Nathan told David, 'but there is one thing you do not know. You are the man who has been unjust. The Lord has made you king of Israel, and saved you from Saul. He has given you everything you wanted, and more.

Why have you not kept the law of God? Why have you committed such an evil deed? You had Uriah killed and took his wife.'

At that moment David saw how blind

he had been, and he began to shake with shame and horror. 'I have sinned before the Lord,' he gasped. 'My guilt is great.'

'You are truly sorry, therefore you will not die,' said Nathan the prophet. 'Because you have broken God's law, however, you have brought great sorrow upon yourself. The son Bathsheba has given you will die. Your joy will be taken from you, and you will not know the pleasure of seeing your son grow up.'

What a terrible judgement God sent upon David! It was worse than if he himself had been slain. David held out his hands to Nathan in an imploring gesture, but Nathan turned silently away.

That very same day Bathsheba's son became ill.

'Lord,' called David, 'do not chide me in anger, do not punish me in indignation. Have mercy on me, my soul is desolate. I am worn out by grief, and my eyes are weakened by sorrow.'

David did not eat or drink, and all night he lay on the ground and begged God's forgiveness. He prayed for his child's health to be restored and poured out tears for poor Uriah. It was all to no avail however, and in seven days the boy died.

David's pain was unbearable, but he praised God's wisdom and justice, all the same. He took his punishment humbly. He, an earthly king, bowed in awe before the King of Heaven. God forgave him, and David once again lived his life according to the laws of God.

David's Sin

The Wisdom of King Solomon

King David had many sons, but only one of them could become king when David died, and he was called Solomon. When David felt the hour of his death approaching, he called Solomon to him and said, 'Listen to the word of God and obey His commandments. Abide by what is written in the Law he gave to Moses, and you will prosper.'

Solomon never forgot his father's advice. He loved the Lord, and he went to bed and rose in the morning with God's name on his lips. One day God appeared to him in his dreams. 'You are pious and pure of heart,' He told him. 'Ask what you want, and I will fulfil your wish.'

'Lord,' Solomon answered humbly, 'you were merciful to my father, and you have shown me great favour also. You have made me king, but I am too young to rule over your people. There are so many of them that they cannot be counted, and I am alone. I do not know whether I am acting according to your will, so I beg you – give me the ability to resolve all disputes, and to distinguish between right and wrong.'

God was pleased with Solomon's reply. 'You did not ask me for long life or riches, or for me to slay your enemy,' He said. 'You wish only to be just, so I will give you great wisdom. You will be wiser than any other, and in addition I will give you what you have not asked for – riches and glory. No king shall compare with you, for I will raise you up above all of them.'

The fame of Solomon's wisdom soon spread to all lands. He spoke thousands of proverbs, and he could speak the language of the trees and the animals. He knew every plant and animal, and could advise or chide as was necessary.

When he saw a lazy man, he said to him, 'Go and look at how the ants live, and learn from them. They have no leader to tell them what to do, but they always manage to find food for themselves. How much longer are you going to lie here? If you sleep a while and doze a while you will be overtaken by want as a country is overrun by a foreign army.'

Then he told a rich man who did not show mercy to a poor man, 'He who has a full stomach may trample on honeycombs, but for the hungry even a bitter food tastes sweet. Go and share your bread.'

When someone spoke too much, he would say, 'The words of a gossip pierce like a sword; wise tongues heal wounds.'

If a man was mean with money, he would say, 'He who is generous will receive gifts from God, but he who is mean will lose out in the end.'

This was how Solomon taught his people. His kingdom prospered, and he, the king of Israel, thanked God for the gift he had received. 'Happy is he who has found wisdom,' he sang, 'happy he who has knowledge. It is worth more than silver, it gives more than gold. It is more precious than pearls, more valuable than jewellery.

Wisdom leads a man to happiness, and his ways are the ways to peace.'

Solomon was asked for advice by great and powerful rulers, but ordinary people came to him too, asking for a just judgment. One day two women came to him. 'My lord,' said the first of them, 'I know you will not allow an injustice, so I beg you to decide our dispute.'

'Speak,' Solomon replied.

The woman took courage and said, 'This woman and I were left alone by our husbands. Since we were lonely, we moved

into the same house. Not long ago I brought a boy into the world, and this woman also gave birth to a son, but he soon died. It happened at night when I was asleep. She crept up to my bed, stole my child who was lying beside me, and put her dead son in his place. When I went to feed the boy in the morning, I saw that he was dead, but when I looked at the child more carefully, I saw it was not mine. This woman stole my child, and I ask only that she return him to me.'

'He who stops up his ears against the cries of a poor man will one day cry out himself, and no one will answer,' said Solomon to the unhappy woman. 'I want to help you, but I must hear the other side of the story. What do you say?' He turned to the other woman.

'What can I say?' asked the woman in tears. 'What you have heard is a lie. My child is alive. It was hers who died! She only came to you to steal my son.'

'It is you who are the liar!' shouted the first woman. 'My child is alive, and yours is dead.'

'No!' cried the second. 'My son lives, and yours is dead!'

The two women began to shout at each other, each accusing the other. Then they asked Solomon to judge who was telling the truth.

Solomon asked them to tell him the whole story once more, but he could not find any new evidence. The women had been alone in the house at the time, and there were no witnesses; the king had to rely on his own wisdom.

'You both claim that the living child is

your own,' he said in a little while, 'and that the dead child belongs to the other. You will have to share the child. Bring me a sword,' he ordered his servants.

The king's servants brought a large, sharp sword, and Solomon said, 'Now cut the living child in two. Each of the women shall have half of it.'

'Wait!' cried the first woman. She fell on her knees before Solomon and begged him, 'My lord, take pity on this innocent child. Better to give him to this woman, than to let him die.'

Then the second woman said, 'You have judged wisely, Solomon. If this child is not to be mine, then no one else shall have him.'

Upon hearing her words Solomon raised his voice, and cried, 'Hear my judgement. The boy belongs to the first woman. Rather than agree to have him killed, she was willing to give him up. She is the real mother.'

When the people heard of this judgement, they were pleased at the wisdom of their king. 'If a king judges the poor wisely, then he is a strong king,' they said. 'May God bless Solomon forever.'

The Wisdom of King Solomon

A Temple for the Lord

Solomon had ruled over the Israelites for several years. During his reign the land had flourished as never before, but Solomon's happiness was not complete. The King of Israel thought of the words the prophet Nathan had once spoken to David, his father. 'When your days are over and you die,' he had said, 'I will raise your successor above all sovereigns, and make his kingdom secure. Your son will build a temple in honour of

151

my holy name. I shall be his Father, and he my most beloved son.'

'God said I was to build him a temple,' thought Solomon to himself, 'and I have not fulfilled His will. The time has come for me to pay back my debt to God.' So he called messengers and said to them, 'Go to the King of Tyre, Hiram, and tell him that the Lord God of Israel has destroyed all my enemies. My rivals take care not to oppose me, so now, in times of peace, I want to build a temple in Jerusalem in honour of God. You, Hiram, shall tell your servants to fell the tall cedars which grow only in your land. I will use them to build the temple, and will pay for them in wheat and oil.'

Hiram was friendly towards Solomon, as he had been towards his father, David. When he heard the King of Israel's wish, he gave orders at once, and his servants set to work. No one was as fast at felling trees as they were. Huge trunks came crushing to the ground; cedars of Lebanon and cypresses left the places they had occupied for hundreds of years. On the seashore Hiram's men tied the trees together to make rafts, and they began the voyage to the Holy Land.

At the same time the sound of axes echoed throughout the mountains of Israel, the crash of falling stones could also be heard in other parts. The most skilful masons cut huge blocks for foundations of the great building. Other workers hewed and smoothed them, and a thousand porters with their heavy burdens transported them to the site of the temple. Solomon gave strict orders: the temple was to be built without using chisels and hammers; no metal tools were used at all. Iron, which had spilt so much blood, was not permitted to touch the walls of God's house.

The work went well, and after seven years the temple, built on the holy mountain Moria, was finished. No one had ever seen such beauty. Solomon had the floors made of cypress planks, while the walls were clad with cedar from floor to ceiling. The finest artists ornamented them with chalices of flowers and garlands, graceful palm trees and heavenly cherubim.

Inside the temple Solomon set aside a shrine for the Ark of the Covenant containing the stone tablets inscribed with God's commandments. The oracle was made entirely of gold, and there were plates of gold on the other walls of the temple. In the oracle Solomon placed two large cherubim, carved out of rare olive wood inlaid with gold. They stretched their wings up and out, as though they had flown to Earth to guard the heavenly treasure once given to Moses.

Solomon also had fashioned for the shrine ten golden candelabras which stood in front of the Ark, and the altar and table of the temple were also of gold. Only the pillars, the stands, the vessels and the priests' implements were made of bronze. Finally the servants took into the temple all the gifts received by Solomon's father David, magnificent objects made of pure gold and silver, which were placed among the treasures of the Lord's house.

Then Solomon called together the people of Israel and cried, 'Let the priests lift the Ark and take it into the Lord's temple!'

The priests did as the king ordered. From the meeting place they took the Ark, which they rested on long poles, as when they had wandered in the desert, in search of the Promised Land. Now the Ark was to lie between the cherubim in the oracle of the temple. The priests entered the innermost shrine with the Ark resting on their shoulders, and left it there. At that instant the temple was filled with a thick cloud. The people saw the glory of God, and Solomon blessed the God of Israel. He knelt before the Lord's altar, raised his hands to heaven, and said, 'Lord our God, there is none but you in Heaven or on Earth. Hear your servants' prayer, hear the words of those who turn to your temple in prayer. If Israel is in need, help her. If she is troubled by hunger, if the

A Temple for the Lord

heavens close and the rain does not fall, take pity on her and grant her your gifts. Take pity on all who seek your mercy, and fill us with love and the fear of your holy name.'

When Solomon had finished his prayer all the people held a great celebration in God's honour. Israel rejoiced for fourteen days, praising its king, and giving thanks to the Lord for all his bounty.

Then God appeared to Solomon again. When the King of Israel fell asleep, he heard the words of God, 'I have heard your prayer, and your wish, Solomon. The temple you have built will be sacred to me, and I will never turn my face away from it.'

Only then did Solomon feel peace and contentment in his heart. He had done as his father, David, before him and lived his life according to God's wishes. God loved Solomon. He granted success to everything he did, and showered him with luxury, the like of which had never been enjoyed by any other living man.

Solomon built himself a palace which

none could match, filled with splendid halls and chambers. In the middle of the Hall of Judgement stood a throne resting on six pillars, and it was there that Solomon sat when he settled arguments among his people. The throne was carved of ivory and inlaid with gold, and on each of its steps there were two lions. Solomon's throne shone like silver, and all who saw it were in awe of it.

One day stood before this throne the Queen of Sheba, the most honoured of all visitors Solomon had ever received. When she had heard of Solomon's riches and wisdom, she rode to Jerusalem in a huge and grand procession. A long caravan of camels carried sweet-scented balsams, gold and precious stones.

'I have heard of the favour you enjoy with God,' the Queen of Sheba told Solomon. 'I should like to see your treasures with my own eyes, and hear your wisdom.'

'I have only to desire anything I can see,' Solomon replied. 'I have built walls around Jerusalem, I have made beautiful gardens and orchards. Reservoirs feed the trees and flowers with water; I have more cattle than any ruler before me. I drink out of golden cups and have more silver than there are stones by the wayside. Caravans and ships bring me gifts; I own a thousand horses, mules, peacocks and apes. I can show you all of this. As for my wisdom, ask what you will.'

The Queen of Sheba spoke with Solomon about all the things which troubled

her, and Solomon gave her much good advice. He solved all the riddles she gave him, and there was no question which he could not answer. The Queen of Sheba left full of praise for Solomon, and his fame grew even greater. People learned his proverbs, and followed the wise teachings of the King of Israel.

One day Solomon said, 'There is no just man in the country who does only good and is without sin.'

These were the words of a prophet. For what Solomon had foretold came true. He had for years been pure in spirit, but in his old age his mind dimmed, and he did not do the will of God as he once had. Women from foreign lands who gathered at his court bowed to false gods and idols, and Solomon did not stop them. He was old and tired, and his words no longer held the strength they once had.

God saw that Solomon no longer served Him with all his heart, and so he surrounded him with powerful opponents. Their hatred choked him worse than an iron collar could, and even Solomon himself was filled with hatred and bitterness. Although he sought comfort, he could find none, and remembering the joy he had once known, his heart was filled with sadness. 'Everything changes,' he said. 'Nothing is forever. So let each one fear God and keep His commandments, for that is the most important thing of all.'

It was the fortieth year of Solomon's reign in Israel. He died in the royal city of Jerusalem, and was buried beside his forefathers.

A Temple for the Lord

The Prophet Elijah and King Ahab

After the deaths of David and Solomon, Israel was a divided land. No sooner was Solomon in his grave than his kingdom was split into two parts. The first of them, to the north, was now called Israel, while the other was called Judea. There were many kings in both lands, but none could match either David's power or Solomon's wisdom. There were more godless kings, those who drove the one God, Lord of Heaven and Earth, from their hearts, than those who were equitable and renowned for their godfearing deeds.

One of these was King Ahab. He did not serve the Lord, and bowed to idols more than any king had before. He took as his wife Jezebel, daughter of the King of Zidon, who worshipped the false god Baal. Ahab had a temple and an altar built to him, and he had a sacred totem raised, as was the custom among nations which did not fear God. In the days of Ahab and Jezebel the land was filled with prophets of Baal, but God's prophets had to go into hiding. Jezebel ordered all those who believed in God to be killed, and many just men died cruel deaths for their belief in God. Only a few prophets survived the persecution, and one of them was Elijah. He was born in Tishbe, and was therefore called the Tishbite.

He had nothing but a leather smock and a hair cloak, but for all of this he felt himself to be the happiest and richest man in the world. His mind was always on God, and he lived for nothing but God's truth. God sent Elijah to Ahab.

'Your guilt is great,' the prophet said to the wicked ruler. 'Therefore, as God lives, there will be no dew and no rain unless I say so.'

Before the king knew what was happening, Elijah was gone. Ahab sent messengers to capture him, but he seemed to have disappeared from the face of the Earth. Time passed by, and Ahab's kingdom was overtaken by great drought. The heavens seemed to have closed their gates, and not a drop of rain fell. Israel suffered for the sins of its proud king and for its own guilt, but Elijah was not affected at all.

'Hide by the stream called Cherith,' God told him. 'I have ordered the rooks to bring you bread and meat, and the stream will give you pure water.'

Many days passed. The rooks brought Elijah food, and the clear water of the stream quenched his thirst, but the Sun beat down fiercely, and the water in the stream began to dry up. When the bed was quite dry and only baked stones were left, Elijah went away to the neighbouring land. He stayed there for three years, and in all that time it did not rain in Israel. The land was overtaken by great poverty. Nothing grew in the fields, the cattle died, and people were so weak they could barely stand. Then Elijah went to Ahab again.

'Are you the prophet who brought down ruin upon Israel?' the king shouted at him.

'It was not I, but you who brought about its doom,' Elijah replied. 'You have abandoned the Lord, and you and your wife Jezebel bow to unholy gods. You have turned Israel away from truth and honesty, and so it is up to me to show them all who the real God is. Gather together all the people. Let them come to Mount Carmel, and let the prophets of Baal come too.'

Ahab, desperate from the drought and the failure of his crops, did not dare go against Elijah. He gave instructions for the Israelites to gather on the day Elijah said, and took them along with the prophets of Baal to Mount Carmel. Elijah went in front of the gathering and called out, 'How long will you jump from one side to the other? How long can you go on worshipping two gods? See, I stand here alone, and there are four hundred and fifty of the prophets of Baal. Slay two bullocks, and place their carcases on pyres. I will stand by one pyre, the prophets of Baal beside the other.

They shall call their gods, and I will turn to the Lord. Whichever of these replies from the heavens and sends fire to light the pyre is the true God, and that one shall you worship.'

'It shall be so,' the people said. 'Let it be done.'

The prophets of Baal were the first to have their pyre ready. They slew a bullock, placed pieces of its meat on the wood they had prepared, and from morning till noon called out the name of Baal. 'Baal, answer us!' they called. 'Baal, answer us!'

'You must shout louder,' Elijah mocked them. 'Perhaps your Baal cannot hear you. Or has he gone away on a long journey? Perhaps he is asleep – you should shout as loud as you can, so as to wake him up.'

The servants of Baal raised their voices even louder. They cut their flesh and smeared themselves with their own blood, so that Baal might hear them, but no one answered their prayers.

Then Elijah said to the people, 'Come to me.'

The Israelites came forward, and Elijah began in front of them to build an altar to the Lord. He took twelve stones, the same number as the tribes of Israel, and raised an altar from them. He placed wood on these stones, and the meat on the wood. 'Lord God of Abraham, Isaac and Jacob,' he called out, 'let it be seen that you are the God of Israel and that I am your servant, who obeys your word. God, answer me, so that the people may honour your name.'

With that, a great fire shot out of the heavens; it breathed its hot breath on them all, burned the wood on the altar and the meat Elijah had offered with it.

When the people saw this, they fell on their knees and cried out, 'The Lord is the one God! The Lord is the one God!'

Then Elijah said to Ahab, 'Go up to the summit of Mount Carmel. I can hear the sound of rain.'

Fearfully, Ahab obeyed. From the top of the mountain he looked out on the countryside, stared at the deep blue sky, and in his spirit said that Elijah must be mistaken for once. 'How could rain fall from a clear sky?' he thought. 'No such miracle has ever happened before.'

Suddenly, on the horizon, he saw a cloud the size of a man's palm appear.

'Come down quickly,' Elijah told Ahab. 'A terrible rainstorm is coming.'

At that moment the heavens clouded over. A wind brought black clouds, and after the long months of drought, it began at last to rain. Streams of water came pouring to Earth. The parched soil sucked in the life-giving rain, and the people rejoiced. God had taken pity on them in their sins; the drought was at an end.

Yet, even after seeing all this, Ahab had not learned his lesson. When, soaked to the skin, he arrived back at his palace, and had recovered a little from the shock, he swore vengeance on Elijah. The prophet had to hide once again from the king's wrath, and Ahab continued to break the Law of God.

The king was not only godless, but

The Prophet Elijah and King Ahab

greedy, too. Not satisfied with a king's riches, he wanted more and more. He was especially envious of a certain Naboth, an honourable man whose vines grew alongside Ahab's palace. 'Why should I look out of my window on someone else's riches?' thought the king. 'I must have those vines for myself.'

So he went to Naboth and told him, 'Sell me your vineyard. I want to make a garden out of it.'

'God forbid that I should sell my inheritance,' Naboth replied. 'This vineyard has been in my family for generations, I cannot give it up.'

Ahab went back to his palace in an angry mood. He told his wife Jezebel what had happened, and she said to him, 'Do not worry. I will get you your vineyard. Wait and see.'

Before the Sun set down, Jezebel wrote a number of letters, and signed them in Ahab's name. Then she put the royal seal on them, and sent them to the elders of the people and the leaders of the land. 'I want Naboth's death,' they said. 'Pay two men to say that he has blasphemed against God and against the king. Then try him and sentence him to death.'

The elders and leaders of the Israelites had been placed in office by Ahab and Jezebel, and were as godless as they. They found two good-for-nothings who were willing to say anything for money; they accused Naboth of the grave sin against God and king. The court called out its

judgement, and Naboth was put to death.

At once Ahab hurried into the poor fellow's vineyard. He took it for himself, and was pleased with the beautiful heavy grapes it produced, the fruit of Naboth's labour.

God was not one to forget the innocent victim, however. 'Go to Ahab in Naboth's vineyard,' he told the prophet Elijah, 'and tell him, "In the place where the dogs licked Naboth's blood, they will lick yours, too."'

Elijah went to Ahab once more and spoke to him.

'You have found me again,' Ahab cried, angrily.

'It is so,' Elijah replied. 'For you are doing great evil. Your fate is sealed, Ahab, and Jezebel, too, shall be punished. Even in death she shall not find peace, for the dogs will tear her flesh. She will never be buried.'

Ahab knew he was hearing the words of God, and he shook with fear. He tore his clothes as a sign of mourning, and waited anxiously for the punishment of God to arrive.

At the time the armies of Israel and Syria were going to battle. Ahab dressed in the clothes of an ordinary soldier, so that his royal armour should not attract the enemy's attention; but it was not a human adversary he was up against. It was the Lord Himself, who guided a Syrian arrow so that it found a chink in the evil king's armour. Ahab fell from his chariot, and when they carried his body out the dogs came to lick the blood that was left behind.

Jezebel, too, died, as God had predicted. On the day her injustices reached their peak, her own courtiers rose up against her. They threw her from a window of the palace, and left her body to the hungry dogs.

Israel was purified again. The godless had been punished as they deserved.

The Prophet Elijah and King Ahab

Elisha – Pupil of Elijah

On his travels through the Holy Land the prophet Elijah had found a pupil. His name was Elisha, and he loved his teacher dearly, following him everywhere and serving him well.

When Elijah grew old, God said to him, 'Your days have been fulfilled, and soon you are to die. I will send a mighty wind, upon which you will rise up to Heaven.'

'Blessed are you, God,' said Elijah. 'Let your will be done.'

Turning to his companion, he said to him, 'Stay here, Elisha, and let me go off on my own. God sends me to Beth-el.'

Elisha's thoughts were close to the Lord, and so he knew what God had spoken to Elijah. 'How can I leave my master alone?' he thought, and he said to Elijah out loud, 'As the Lord lives and as you live, I will not leave you. I will go too.'

So they went together until they came to Beth-el. No sooner had they entered the town than the prophets who lived there came out to meet them. They, too, knew what was to happen, and they addressed Elisha at once, 'Do you know that this day the Lord is to call your master to Heaven?'

'I know what you know,' Elisha replied sadly. 'Why are you not silent?'

The prophets went away and Elijah

turned to his pupil for a second time. 'The Lord sends me to Jericho,' he said. 'Stay here – I will go on my own.'

'As the Lord lives and as you live, I will not leave you. I will go too,' Elisha replied a second time.

So they went on their way until they reached Jericho. At the gate of the city other prophets were waiting for them. 'Elisha,' they said to Elijah's pupil, just as the prophets of Beth-el had done, 'we have been told that this day the Lord will take your master into Heaven.'

'He revealed this to me, too,' Elisha told them, his head hung low. 'It would be better if you did not speak about it.'

So he turned away from the prophets,

and Elijah said to him a third time, 'Stay here, Elisha. God sends me to the River Jordan.'

'As the Lord lives and as you live, I will not leave you. I will go too,' Elisha replied firmly.

He joined his master and strode alongside him until they reached the banks of the river. There Elijah took off his cloak, rolled it up, and struck the water with it as if with a rod. The moment the cloak struck the surface, the waters parted. In the place where a few moments before there had been running water, there was now a strip of sand and stones, a narrow path from one bank to the other.

'Soon God will part you and me,' Elijah told his pupil, when they got to the other bank of the Jordan. 'Tell me what I can do for you.'

'Let a double portion of your prophet's spirit rest upon me,' Elisha requested.

'It is not me, but God who decides this,' Elijah told him. 'If you see me rise up into Heaven, it shall be as you wish. If I am hidden from your eyes, God will not grant this gift to you.'

After these words the two of them took leave of each other. They were still speaking when a fiery chariot drawn by fiery horses came down from Heaven. The flames glowed in Elijah's face, separating Elisha from his teacher. A great wind got up, grabbed Elijah, and he, the chariot and

Elisha – Pupil of Elijah

the horses suddenly disappeared high in the sky.

'Father!' cried Elisha sorrowfully. 'Father!'

All to no avail, for Elijah was in this world no more. All he left behind him was the picture of the prophet rising to Heaven in Elisha's mind, and his cloak which had slipped from his shoulders, on to the ground.

As a sign of mourning, Elisha tore apart his own cloak and dressed in that of Elijah. Slowly, he set off back towards the Jordan. On the banks of the river he struck the water with the cloak, as Elijah had done before. The river divided to let him pass. God had granted Elisha's wish. The spirit of the prophet Elijah had entered his pupil.

From that day on Elisha wandered through Judea, and everywhere he went he worked miracles and deeds of wonder.

When the land was troubled by bad water, so that nothing grew in the fields, Elisha threw a handful of salt into a well and prayed to the Lord. The water ceased doing harm, and the fields grew green.

On another occasion Elisha visited a woman who was in trouble. Her husband had died, and the poor creature did not know how she was to pay her debts. 'If I do not pay them,' she wailed, 'the one I am in debt to will take both my children.'

'Have you any property?' asked Elisha.

'Only a vessel full of oil,' the woman replied.

'Go and borrow as many empty vessels as you can from your neighbours,' Elisha told her. 'Bring them home and put the oil from your vessel into each of them until they are full. There will be enough, do not worry.'

The woman did as Elisha told her. That day she sold so much oil that she was able to pay off her debt, and had some money left over to live on.

In another part of the Holy Land a man brought Elisha twenty pieces of barley bread.

'Give them to the poor,' Elisha told him.

'There are only twenty pieces,' the stranger replied, 'and there are at least a hundred hungry ones.'

'Do as I tell you, and give out the bread,' Elisha told him. 'Did not God say, "They will eat, and there will be some left over?"'

So the man did as he was told, and indeed all those who were hungry ate their fill, and there was still some bread left for the next time.

So, in this way, Elisha was a helper and a protector to his people, and he became an envoy of justice and love, like the prophet Elijah.

At the time Elisha was wandering the Holy Land, the Israelites were under threat from the King of Aramea. His general, Naaman, was held in great favour by the king, but he was not satisfied with his life. Naaman was troubled by a terrible disease. Leprosy disfigured his face and body, and no one knew how to cure him.

Now Naaman's wife had a servant girl

who was born in the Holy Land. 'If your master were to go to the prophet Elisha, he would surely be cured,' she told her mistress one day.

As soon as Naaman heard about this, he went before his king and told him everything.

'I will send a letter to the King of Israel,' the Aramean king said. 'Let the Israelites cure you.'

When the King of Israel, Joram, son of Ahab and Jezebel, received this message from the Arameans, he was filled with great fear. He was not such a sinner as his father and mother, but he was not godly, either. He did not rule according to the laws of God, and lived in fear of the day when God would send a foreign army to shake the foundations of his dynasty and his land.

'Am I the Lord, to deal out life and death,' he lamented over the letter from the King of Aramea. 'I have no idea how to cure Naaman. The Arameans are just looking for an excuse to attack and destroy us.'

Elisha heard of the king's fears, and he sent him a message. 'Send Naaman to me. I will show him that there is still a prophet of God in Israel.'

It was not long before Naaman's chariot, drawn by choice horses, was standing outside Elisha's house.

'Go and wash seven times in the River Jordan,' Elisha told the Aramean general. 'You will become clean, and your body will be healthy again.'

Naaman was furious. 'Is that all the advice you can give me, when I have come all this way?' he cried. 'Are there not enough rivers in my own land in which I can wash?'

Offended, he turned to leave, and would have driven away, only his servants said to him, 'Naaman, do as you are told. Did not Elisha tell you, "Wash; and you shall be pure." He will surely help you.'

Naaman hesitated. 'Very well,' he thought. 'I will do as Elisha asks; but if my disease is not cured, the Jews will know the wrath of the Aramean army.'

Carefully, Naaman stepped into the River Jordan and submerged himself seven times. When he had done so, his fearful disease was cured. His deformed skin was healed, becoming as smooth and firm as that of a boy.

That day Elisha saved Israel from destruction. God governed his actions, and filled Naaman's heart with humility and awe. 'I have seen that there is no God like the God of Israel,' he said.

Now Naaman no longer wanted to fight the people of God. He went home to his own land and the prophet Elisha continued to do the will of the Lord.

The Lesson
of Jonah

After the death of Elisha, God called upon other prophets to explain his word. One of these was called Jonah. God said to him, 'Jonah, go to the city of Nineveh, which is far away from here. Call together its inhabitants, and tell them I will not countenance their sins any longer. They are deceitful, they are thieves and murderers.'

Jonah was greatly startled. 'What is God asking of me?' he thought. 'Nineveh is the city of the Assyrians, the Israelites' greatest enemies. They worship the god Ishtar, and do not fear the one true God. If I tell them the message of God in Nineveh they will laugh at me. Perhaps they will even grow angry and kill me. No, I will go nowhere,' he decided. 'I will run away from God. Let the Assyrians in Nineveh lie, steal and kill. It will be better if they do not repent, and God destroys them.'

So Jonah set out at once. Nineveh was to the west, but he set out towards the east. In the port of Joppa he found a ship that was sailing to the distant port of Tarsis. He paid the master of the ship for his passage. The ship set sail and before long it was surrounded by open sea. 'I have done the right thing,' thought Jonah, 'to come out to sea. God will not look for me here.'

No sooner had these thoughts come to Jonah than the heavens clouded over. Black clouds covered the sky, and a strong wind raised high seas. A great storm was unleashed by God. Flashes of lightning split the waves, and thunder roared, as though the ground itself were cracking open beneath the sea.

The sailors were seized with terror. They prayed to their own gods, begging to be spared, but their lamenting did nothing to calm the waves. The storm only raged fiercer than ever, and the ship was threatened with shipwreck. They threw the whole cargo overboard, hoping that when the ship was lightened in this way it might be able to weather the storm. All their efforts were in vain, however. The ship bobbed to and fro in the midst of the waves,

creaking and groaning, as if it were about to split in two. The sailors did not know what to do.

Meanwhile Jonah, frightened for his life, had gone deep below decks. He curled up in the darkest corner of the ship, and tried to go to sleep. 'A storm like this is no accident,' he thought. 'If only I might sleep through God's anger.'

The sailors did not let him sleep, however. 'Get up,' they said, shaking him.

'Why are you hiding? Say who you are, and why you do not ask your own God for help!'

Jonah was silent. He was afraid to admit that he was fleeing from God. He did not wish them to know that the storm was all his fault.

Then the sailors drew lots to find out who had brought such misfortune down upon them. The lot fell on Jonah. Now he could deny it no longer. 'I am a Jew,' he told them. 'I fear the Lord, God of the heavens, who created the sea and the land. He has sent His anger upon me, because I did not obey His command. I wanted to run away from God, but now I know there is nowhere to run to. You would die in vain on my account. Throw me overboard, and the storm will subside.'

The sailors did not want to do as Jonah asked. They sat down to the oars and rowed with new strength, to try to reach land. Yet however hard they tried, they could not overcome the stormy seas. With a heavy heart they did as Jonah had asked. They threw him overboard, and at that instant God's anger passed. The seas went down, and the waves ceased to beat against the side of the ship.

Jonah vanished beneath the surface of the water and fell to the bottom of the sea. He thought he was going to die, but God did not let him escape. He sent along a huge fish, a monster such as no man had ever seen. It opened its great jaws and swallowed Jonah before he knew what was happening.

It was only then that Jonah began to regret not having obeyed God's will. He grieved that he would never see a human face again, or the trees and flowers, and begged God's forgiveness. 'I will go to Nineveh,' he promised. 'I will keep my word.'

When God heard Jonah's mourning, He told the fish to swim to the shore. After three days and nights Jonah was thrown up on the dry land.

Then God said to Jonah, 'Go through the sinful city of Nineveh from end to end, and cry out everywhere you go, "In forty days' time you will be destroyed!"'

This time Jonah did as the Lord told him. Nineveh was a large city. To get from one side to the other took three days, but Jonah did not regret the effort, and day and night he announced the fate which awaited the Ninevehans. He spoke to thieves and murderers. He warned the rich, who did not take pity on the homeless children. He persuaded the proud merchants, who drove beggars from their doors. He stopped on every street, at every house, and when he had thus fulfilled the will of the Lord, he went up on to the heights overlooking the city, from where he could see the whole of it. There he built a shelter of four bare walls without a roof, and looked down to see how God would punish Nineveh.

But the inhabitants of Nineveh took Jonah's words to heart. When he told them the strange way he had arrived there, they were very startled. They became afraid of the power of God, and decided to mend their ways. The thief gave back what he had stolen. He who had wounded helped to heal. Men, women, young and old fasted. They laid down their fine garments and dressed in hair shirts to punish themselves. In tears they confessed their sins, promising to be better. The King of Nineveh himself left his magnificent throne, took off his cloak embroidered with gold, and along with the people begged God to forgive them.

God knew that the regret of the Ninevehans was genuine, and when the forty days were over, he did not destroy the city.

The Lesson of Jonah

Because of this Jonah became very angry. Forgetting how God had forgiven his own guilt, he cried in rage, 'God, why do you not keep your word? Why have you spared Nineveh? I thought these sinners would soften your heart! Therefore I did not want to go to Nineveh, so that I might not make a fool of myself. I warned them of your wrath, and you have forgiven them! You make me look like a liar!'

Jonah grew quite red with anger. He stamped crossly around his shelter, looking bitterly towards the sleeping city.

God heard the words of Jonah and decided to teach him a lesson. While Jonah was asleep, He had a beautiful ivy overgrow the hovel. It was so thick that it joined together over Jonah's head like a roof. In the morning he woke up, and when he saw the ivy, he forgot his anger. The green leaves protected him from the rays of the Sun, and he spent the whole day giving thanks for the shade the plant

gave him. In the evening he lay on the ground and went to sleep contentedly.

That night God sent a large worm to gnaw at the ivy. As quickly as it had grown, it now withered away. When Jonah woke up, the plant was dry, and the Sun beat down so mercilessly on him that he was quite faint from the heat. 'God!' he cried resentfully. 'What is this supposed to mean? Have you created me to laugh at me? You sent me to Nineveh to tell of its destruction, and then you took pity on the city. Now you have destroyed my ivy!'

God heard the words of Jonah and replied, 'There is no need to be angry, Jonah. You miss the ivy which grew by my will. You neither planted it nor watered it, but you are mourning its loss. Therefore I, who created all men, am not to take pity on them? How could I destroy Nineveh, a great city full of men, women and children? Remember, Jonah. I wish no one's death. I have love for all creatures.'

From then on God never spoke to Jonah again, but Jonah never forgot God's wonders to the end of his days.

Bold Judith

People came into the world and died, and generation followed generation; only God was constant, remaining with His people. He had taken them to the Holy Land, and He blessed them when they followed His will. Yet when they went against the Lord's laws, He punished them. So God sent punishment to the northern part of the Holy Land, delivering it into the hands of enemies. He left only Judea to the Israelites, but soon a mighty enemy led by the terrible Holofernes rose up against them.

He had so many warriors that they could not be counted. They flooded over the land like locusts, wielding lances, swords, slings and bows. With Holofernes's war chariots and riders came slaves driving innumerable sheep, cattle and goats for food, and a herd of camels, donkeys and mules carried his rich spoils. Wherever Holofernes went, cries and weeping went up to heaven. Kings shook before him, and the Israelites of Judea were also afraid. They did not want to give up without a struggle, however, so they guarded all the routes and hilltops, strengthened the ramparts of their cities, and laid by supplies.

Their hands made fortresses, but their minds were with the Lord. 'God,' they called out to Him, 'your holy city of Jerusalem is in danger, and destruction threatens the sacred temple of Solomon. Do not leave us at the mercy of pagans; spare our wives and children!'

When Holofernes found out that the Israelites were making their cities strong, he was very angry. 'How dare they oppose me?' he roared. 'They have not knelt before me like other nations, they have not come out to meet me with gifts, and so I will destroy them. The ground will soak up their blood, and the rivers carry off their bodies. It is no use their relying on that god of theirs. I shall easily conquer them: they will soon see whose is the power and the glory.'

Holofernes's army descended on Judea like a wild flood, driving all before it until it reached the city of Bethulia, high in the mountains. Holofernes besieged the city so that no one could get in or out. Then he called the captains and they held a council to decide how to take it.

'It is difficult to fight in the mountains, and many men will die,' said one of his captains, 'but I know of a weapon which no one can resist. Let us take the spring at the foot of the mountains and lead the water off in another direction. The Israelites will be so weakened by thirst and hunger that they will fall before they even draw their swords.'

These words of cunning pleased Holofernes. He dammed the spring so that not a drop of water got through to the citizens, and then waited patiently for the Isrealites in Bethulia to use up all their supplies.

After thirty-four days the water tanks of the besieged city were dry. The Israelites were growing weak with thirst and hunger, and their trembling hands could scarcely hold weapons. All the people gathered together before Uzijah, the chief elder of the city, and wept, crying out, 'What have we done to deserve this? It was better to surrender to Holofernes. Better to be a slave than to die like this in want. God has turned His face away from us. We are abandoned and condemned.'

'Do not lose heart,' Uzijah encouraged them. 'Continue to beg God for mercy, and He will save us. We must hold out for another five days. If help does not come by then, I swear we shall open the gates of the city. We will bow before Holofernes, and give ourselves up to his mercy.'

One of those who heard these words was Judith, widow of Menas of the Simeon tribe, a kind and beautiful woman. She looked after large herds and fields on her own, gave orders to many servants, and kept a large house. Judith feared God with all her heart, and she kept His laws and spoke wisdom and truth.

When Uzijah left the meeting of the people, Judith sent her chambermaid to bring him to her along with the elders of the city. The men came to her house, and

Bold Judith

she told them, 'You spoke ill, Uzijah, and you risk God's wrath. Why did you swear to give the city over to the enemy, if help does not arrive within five days? Is it not in God's power to save us even after that? Could He not slay us today, if He so wished? Man cannot decide how God should act; only the Lord is our master. Let us pray to Him and give thanks for the trials He has sent upon us. Let us call out His name, and defend our city and our lives.'

Uzijah bowed his head. 'I have done wrong,' he said. 'The people persuaded me, which is why I made the oath, but you, Judith, are beloved of God. Pray for rain to fill our vessels; beg God to give our people the strength to fight.'

'I will do more than this,' replied Judith, 'and all generations will remember it. Tonight I will go to Holofernes's camp. Be-

fore five days are over, the Lord will bring salvation to Bethulia through me. Ask nothing, do not try to find anything out. When the time is ripe you shall know everything.'

That night Judith spoke to the Lord for a long time. 'God,' she said, from the depth of her heart, 'take heed of our suffering; we are exhausted from our hardships. You are the God of the humbled, the helper of the lowest, defender of the weak, protector of the despairing. Lord of Heaven and Earth, Creator of the waters, King of all creation, hear my prayer!'

Then Judith put scented ointments on her body and dressed in her finest robes. She tied her hair in a band, put bracelets on her arms and rings on her fingers, and

hung earrings from her ears. As silent as a ghost she crossed Bethulia and left the city. She made her way towards Holofernes's sentries, in order to fight alone with the enemies of Israel.

Soon Judith came across Holofernes's soldiers. 'I am from the nation of Israel, and I am fleeing a city which has fallen victim to death,' she told them. 'I came out to show your general a secret way into the city. Whoever takes that route may become master of the city and of the mountain stronghold.'

Holofernes's soldiers were captivated by Judith's beauty and fascinated by her words. They took her to Holofernes, and he, too, was astounded. Her beauty daz-

zled his eyes, and he listened in enchantment to her voice.

'We are a strange people,' Judith told the general of the enemy army. 'We are people close to the one God. If we keep His laws, no army will overcome us. It has come about that the people of Bethulia have lost their heads. Hunger and thirst have crazed them; they demand grain, wine and oil which is holy and reserved for the priests of God. The Lord will not let this guilt go unpunished. He will send death to these sinners; so, Holofernes, allow me now to pray to my God. He will tell me when the Israelites have fallen victim to sin, and your victory will be assured. I will show you the way into the city.'

Bold Judith

Holofernes and his servants were like men bewitched. They believed Judith, and Holofernes promised her great honours. He allowed her to move freely through the camp and no one was to disturb her at prayer. Three times she left the camp, and in the silence of night asked for the Lord's help.

On the fourth day Holofernes held a great feast in his tent. All his captains came, and they ate and drank long into the night. When Holofernes had become drunk with wine, he sent for Judith. 'Feast with me,' he said, 'and stay near to me. When the others have gone, stay here. I want to look upon your beauty until the Sun comes up.'

Late in the night the feast came to an end. The captains went to their own tents and a servant drew the curtains on Holofernes's couch. The general was asleep. The heavy wine had overcome him, and he lay helpless on a skin, as if all life had left him.

This was the moment Judith had been waiting for. 'O God,' she prayed, 'give me strength and guide my hand.' From the pillar beside his couch she took the general's sword and struck him twice in the neck. His head fell to the ground. The terrible warrior was dead.

Judith put the head in a bag and left the tent quietly. The soldiers took no notice of her, thinking she was going out to pray again, but Judith hurried back along the same path she had taken a few days ago.

Before daybreak she stood before the gates of Bethulia. 'Open up, brothers,' she called. 'God is with us; He has shown His strength over our enemy.'

The defenders recognized Judith's voice and opened the gate. Torches lit up the woman and the bag she held in her hand.

'See,' she called out. 'It is the head of Holofernes. Through my hand God has slain the leader of our enemies.'

News of this heroic deed spread through the whole city. Men again stood strong and firm as though new blood coursed through their veins. The story of Judith's bravery gave the Israelites new strength, and each one of them made ready to fight.

When the Sun rose in the morning, Holofernes's soldiers saw the head of their leader on the ramparts of Bethulia. Horrified, they ran to Holofernes's tent. On his couch lay his headless body, and beside it his own sword.

The huge army lost courage at once. 'A woman has humbled us,' cried the soldiers. 'We are mocked and shamed.'

At that moment the defenders of Bethulia attacked. With resolute force they struck at the disarrayed ranks of the enemy, putting them to flight. The Israelites struck down the marauders, pursued and caught them, and won glorious victory. Then they sang Judith's praises, thanking her for saving them, and wrote songs of gratitude and love to their God.

Daniel

Many rulers' names are written in the memory of the people of Israel. Some were such as they could be proud of, others brought shame on the Jews. But the godlessness of Jehoiakim, King of Judea, brought unhappiness on the whole people.

Jehoiakim profaned the temple of Solomon, built in honour of God. He filled it with images of pagan gods, and forced his people to worship the sun, the moon and the stars instead of the one true God. The

land blessed by God fell into the power of evil. The Israelites disobeyed the word of the Lord, and the messengers of God who tried to preach it were showered with mockery and insults.

When God saw that His people had taken no notice of the warnings they had received, He grew very angry. 'I will punish this nation for its injustice,' He said. 'My wrath shall descend upon them.' He brought a great army in from the north, and it conquered the rest of the Holy Land, Judea. The city of Jerusalem was looted, and the ruler of the raiders, Nebuchadnezzar, entered Solomon's temple. He took the sacred vessels and many treasures and slaves and sent them back to his own country, Babylonia.

Among the slaves was Daniel, a handsome young man, gifted with wisdom and knowledge. Though many people in his land did not fear God, he still loved the Creator and God gave him the gift of understanding dreams and visions, a secret which is hidden from ordinary people. Nebuchadnezzar was impressed by Daniel's learning, and when one day he explained a dream which none of the Babylonian seers could understand, he made Daniel chief of his counsellors.

Daniel remained at the court of Nebuchadnezzar even after his death, and served his successors. One of these was Nebuchadnezzar's son Belshazzar, a very proud and arrogant man. One day he held a great feast, to which he invited a thousand noblemen. Belshazzar drank a lot of

wine, and when he grew drunk he gave orders for food and drink to be brought in the sacred gold and silver vessels stolen from the temple in Jerusalem. This was done at once, and Belshazzar and his subjects began praising their iron, wooden and stone idols, which had given them victory over the God of the Jews. No sooner had the Babylonians tasted food from the sacred vessels, however, than something unexpected happened. Before all their eyes the fingers of a human hand appeared, and not very far from the king wrote something on the wall. Nobody could be seen, but only the hand, moving in the air.

Belshazzar was filled with terror. His face paled and his knees shook. He called for his sorcerers in a voice filled with fear. 'Whoever reads this writing and explains the words to me, shall become my favourite,' he said. 'I will dress him in crimson, place my golden chain around his neck, and raise him above all others.'

On the king's orders all the most revered of Babylonia's wise men and soothsayers gathered together, but they said nothing to Daniel. They hoped they would be able to explain this sign themselves, and in this way make Daniel less important. When the Babylonian seers saw the secret writing, though, they were as baffled as Belshazzar himself. They looked at each other in confusion, and finally said, 'Our skills are not sufficient to explain this, my lord.'

Then the queen noticed that Daniel was

not among them. 'Do not despair, my lord,' she told Belshazzar. 'There is one more man here, an immigrant from Judea, whose wisdom is beyond that of all the other wise men. He is the one you should ask.'

So Belshazzar called Daniel and showed him the inscription. 'I have heard you are able to reveal all mysteries,' he said. 'If you explain these words to me, I will reward you richly.'

'I do not want your gifts,' Daniel said. 'Just listen to what God, Lord of all living things, is telling you. In His mercy He gave you a kingdom, glory and dignity. He raised you above other mortals, but you did not praise the true God. You feasted from the vessels which once stood in His sacred house, and you praised your own gods of iron, wood and stone. Therefore God has given you a sign, and the fingers of the mysterious hand have written invisible words. Only God and I know what is written there. *Mene, tekel, upharsin* is what is written in the Hebrew tongue – counted, weighed up, divided. God has counted the days of your rule, weighed up your pride and arrogance, and will divide your kingdom between the Medes and the Persians.'

When Daniel had finished speaking, he left. That very night Medean rebels rose up against Belshazzar. They killed the proud king and put their own ruler, Darjavesh, on the throne. God's words were fulfilled, and Belshazzar's reign came to an end.

The new ruler, Darjavesh, also left Daniel at his court. He, too, was soon to realize what a special man he was. He wanted to make Daniel steward of his entire kingdom. The royal sages and officials were upset. The seers had not forgotten the embarrassment they had suffered through Daniel's wisdom, and the officials were afraid they might lose their privileges. So they got together and agreed that they must prevent Daniel from becoming the second most powerful man in the country. At first they tried to accuse him of being a bad adviser to the king, but try as they might, they could find nothing against him. They said to themselves, 'Daniel is honest, he neither steals nor deceives. We must find another excuse; we must use that God of his.'

So they gathered around the king and began to entreat him. 'Great Darjavesh,' they said, 'we are thinking of your own good. We have an idea. Issue an order that all who worship any god or man but you will be thrown into a pit filled with hungry lions.'

Since Darjavesh liked to be honoured, he agreed, but Daniel had always worshipped in the ways of Israel. Three times a day he turned to the holy city of Jerusalem and with pleas and thanks on his lips he prayed to his Creator. When Darjavesh signed the ominous decree, Daniel continued as before. He still paid homage to his God, and this was just what his enemies were waiting for. Quickly they went to Darjavesh and told him of Daniel's practices.

'Sire,' they cried, 'Daniel of the Jewish immigrants obeys neither you nor your laws. He prays to his God, and so you must throw him to the lions. You are a mighty ruler, and you, too, must keep your word!'

Darjavesh grew sad. He liked Daniel, and did not want to harm him, but as king of a mighty empire he must not appear to be weak. He thought desperately how he might save Daniel. Even by the time darkness had fallen, he had still not thought of anything. He had signed the decree, and now he could not go back on that. With a heavy heart he agreed to do as Daniel's enemies asked. He called Daniel in and said, 'You have disobeyed my orders, and so you will be thrown to the hungry lions. May the God you believe in so save you.'

Then the guards took Daniel and threw him into a stone cell filled with savage creatures. The soldiers blocked the entrance with a stone, and on it they placed the seal of King Darjavesh and his nobles, so that no one might set Daniel free.

That night Darjavesh had a heavy heart. He turned down all the usual entertainments; he would neither eat, nor drink, and for a long time he could not sleep. At dawn he hurried to the lions' den into which Daniel had been thrown. 'Daniel,' he called sadly, 'has your God saved you?'

'I am alive, my lord,' came Daniel's voice from deep inside. 'God saw that I had done no evil, and would not allow me to die. He sent His angel to me, and he kept back the terrible lions. They have not hurt me at all.'

Darjavesh rejoiced. He told the guards to take Daniel out of the cell, and to his amazement saw that he was indeed untouched. It was only now that the king realized the evil noblemen had tricked him. They were not interested in him or in his glory, but only wished to be rid of Daniel.

'Let the wicked counsellors meet the fate they wished upon Daniel,' he ordered.

Before the envious officials even touched the bottom of the stone pit, the lions began to tear them to pieces, and ground their bones between their teeth. Darjavesh then gave orders that were ceremoniously decreed throughout the land. 'Let all fear the God of Daniel, for He is the living God and is eternal, and His kingdom has no end. He delivers and protects, performs miracles in Heaven and on Earth.'

So God rewarded Daniel for his faithfulness. After that Daniel prospered until Darjavesh's death, and his successor, the Persian king, Kyros, was Daniel's protector. Out of reverence to the God of Israel, he allowed the Jews to return from Babylonia to their own country. The seventy year exile of the Jews ended, and the descendants of Abraham, Isaac and Jacob again became lords of their own land. Even in years to come they spoke of Daniel, the man who although in the greatest of danger did not cease to believe in the God of his forefathers.

Esther, who Saved the Jews

Under King Kyros many of the Jews returned to their homeland, but even more of them remained in far off lands. Many lived in the Persian Empire. The Persians were hardy warriors and skilful rulers. Their power grew steadily, and when King Ahasuerus came to the throne, he ruled over one hundred and twenty-seven lands from distant India to the deserts of Arabia.

185

It happened that Ahasuerus drove away his wife Vashti in anger, and the land was left without a queen. After some time, when the king's rage subsided, the courtiers said to him, 'Great ruler, it is not good for you to be alone. Let the officers in all provinces of the lands of Persia gather together the most beautiful young women and send them to your palace. Whichever takes your fancy shall wear the crown of Queen Vashti.'

Ahasuerus was pleased with the idea. He gave orders, and before long the first

beautiful young women began to arrive at his palace.

At that time there lived not far from the royal palace an old man named Mordecai, a descendant of the Jews who had been driven from the Holy Land. He was a good man, and faithful to the God of Israel and His laws. Mordecai had no one in the whole world except for his foster child, Esther. He had taken care of her when her parents died, and since then he had looked after her as though she were his own daughter. He taught her to love her people and their Lord, and to serve Him.

Esther was very beautiful and graceful. Before long even Ahasuerus's messengers had heard of her beauty, as they went about the land looking for a new queen, so they summoned Esther to the palace.

Before Esther left, Mordecai said to her,

'When you come to the palace, do not say you are one of our people. Pray in secret, and do not let them know which God you believe in.'

Esther said goodbye to Mordecai and went before the king. When Ahasuerus saw her, she at once gained his favour and attention. He loved her more than all the other women, and made her queen instead of Vashti.

While Esther lived at the palace, Mordecai would sit at the royal gate. There he could hear what the people talked of, and he knew their hearts and their ways. One day he heard two of Ahasuerus's courtiers plotting against their king. He told Esther, and she warned the king. Before the conspirators could carry out their plans they were imprisoned and punished. Then the royal scribe wrote in the chronicle that Mordecai had saved the king's life, and Mordecai did not mind receiving no greater honour than this. As ever, he bowed to the Lord thrice daily and with the words of his ancestors thanked Him for His bounty.

The more Mordecai was modest, the prouder was one Haman, Ahasuerus's counsellor. He curried favour with the king so skilfully that the Persian ruler raised him above all the lords of the empire. Ahasuerus's servants paid as much respect to Haman as they did to the king himself. Whenever Haman passed them, they would fall on their knees and bow down low. Only Mordecai remained upright, and Haman hated him for it. He only

bowed his head in prayer. When Haman heard from his confidants that Mordecai was a Jew, his hatred grew even stronger. 'I will show you,' he thought. 'I will take vengeance not only on you, but also on your proud people.'

One night Haman called together his counsellors, soothsayers and seers. 'Cast lots,' he told them. 'Let the gods decide which day is destined for the destruction of the Jews.'

In the end the lot fell on the thirteenth day of the twelfth month, known as *adar*. Haman went before Ahasuerus and said, 'Great king, there is a race of people in your land which is spread out, separated from the other peoples. They do not follow the royal laws and keep their own. These foreigners are of no use to you at all, so you should place your seal on an order to have them destroyed. In doing so you will gain great spoils, a great deal of silver and other riches.'

'The silver and the people are yours,' Ahasuerus told him, not knowing that Esther was a Jew. 'Do with them as you see fit.'

The next day speedy messengers went through the whole of Persia, carrying with them letters which bore the royal seal. On the appointed day all Jews, from the smallest baby to the oldest folk, were to be killed. Haman was triumphant; the Jews mourned and lamented. They went to work with tears in their eyes, and with tears in their eyes they left their work at night, weeping, wailing, and counting

Esther, who Saved the Jews

the days until the terrible month arrived.

The terrifying news reached Esther. She was filled with worry; her breath caught in her throat, and she could not think what to do. Then a messenger came to her. 'Esther,' he said, 'I come straight from Mordecai. He tore his cloak as a sign of mourning, sits on the ground in the hair shirt of a penitent, and pours ashes on hair. He prays you and challenges you: Speak to the king; speak for your people. This is our only hope.'

'How am I to do it?' Esther answered sadly. 'I have not seen the king for thirty days, and without his permission I cannot enter his chambers. If I did, I should be put

to death. Only if he caught sight of me and beckoned with his sceptre would I be left alive.'

The messenger left, but soon returned with a new message from Mordecai. 'Go to the king; it may be that you have been made queen just so that you might help your unfortunate people at this moment.'

'Very well,' Esther replied, boldly. 'I will go to the king. Let all the Jews fast. Let them not eat or drink for three days, and beg God's mercy. I will fast, too. Then I will go before the king, and if I am to die, so be it.'

After three days Esther dressed in her royal robes and with her head bowed low, entered the royal chambers. Ahasuerus looked at her, and then beckoned with his sceptre. 'Esther,' he called, 'what is the matter with you? Tell me your wish. If you were to ask for half the kingdom, I should grant it to you.'

'If the king sees fit,' Esther replied humbly, 'let him come to a feast I wish to hold today for him and his counsellor Haman.'

'It shall be so,' Ahasuerus replied.

Haman was very pleased. 'The king and queen favour me greatly,' he boasted to his wife Zeresh. 'They will surely agree to Mordecai being killed this very day. Build a gallows for him!'

In the evening the king, Haman and Esther sat down to the feast. Ahasuerus did not let Esther out of his sight. 'Queen,' he said, 'your face is pale; you are sad and troubled. I would give half my kingdom to know what troubles you.'

188

'Let your majesty be patient,' Esther replied. 'I will hold another banquet for you and Haman tomorrow. There I will tell you everything.'

That night Ahasuerus could not sleep. He had candles lit and the servants read chronicles to him. When they reminded him of how Mordecai had foiled the plot against him, the king asked, 'What reward did he receive?'

'None,' came the reply.

Just at that moment Haman asked for an audience. He wanted to persuade the king to have Mordecai hanged at once, but before he could speak, Ahasuerus said, 'How

am I to reward a man whom I wish to honour?'

The proud Haman thought that the king was speaking about him, and he said at once, 'Let him be dressed in royal robes. Let him sit on a royal steed, let a royal crown be placed upon his head, and let

a royal noblemen lead the horse through the streets calling out, "This is how the king rewards those he wishes to honour!"'

'Go quickly,' the king ordered Haman, 'and do as you have said with Mordecai, who sits by the palace gate.'

Haman could do nothing but obey. Pale with anger, he dressed Mordecai in royal robes, put Ahasuerus's crown upon his head, and helped him into the saddle of the king's horse. Then he went around the city with Mordecai, calling out the words, just as Ahasuerus had ordered.

Haman returned home, humbled and shamed. He had scarcely had time to tell his wife of his disgrace, when the king's courtiers came to him to take him to Esther's feast.

Esther was again silent and sad.

'Queen,' Ahasuerus said gently, 'tell me what is the matter. You may ask half my kingdom, if you wish.'

Then Esther stood up, and with faltering voice said, 'If I enjoy the king's favour, let him spare my life only. If he wishes to give me gifts, let him give me the lives of my people. For we have been sentenced without guilt to a terrible death, from the youngest to the oldest.'

'Who has dared do such a thing?' cried Ahasuerus.

'This man, an adversary and enemy of the whole Jewish nation,' said Esther, pointing to Haman. 'Know you that I and Mordecai, who saved your life, are also of that nation. Haman slandered us, and you have decreed a cruel punishment on us.'

As soon as Ahasuerus heard about the cunning way in which Haman had him sign the decree against the Jews, he grew terribly angry. He called his soldiers and told them to hang Haman on the gallows which he had prepared for Mordecai.

Then Ahasuerus sent a new letter out throughout the land, again bearing the royal seal. In it he gave the Jews the right to defend themselves against any who tried to harm them on the thirteenth day of *adar*.

The enemies of the Jews in the Persian Empire were filled with awe and fear. When the day of trial came, none of them was fortunate in battle. The Jews were victorious over all who rose up against them, and they rejoiced in God's deliverance of their people. They danced and sang, praising the bold queen Esther and the wise Mordecai.

The New Testament

The Message of the Angel Gabriel

Centuries passed and to the west of Jerusalem the Roman Empire grew. The Romans occupied the neighbouring countries and soon became masters of the land where God's people had settled too. On to David's throne the Roman Emperor placed the cruel and ruthless King Herod and Roman traders brought heathen customs to the Jewish towns. These were sad times. Some Jews abandoned the Lord and took on heathen ways. Those who remained true to God, however, placed their hope in the early coming of the Messiah of which their forefathers had spoken. 'He will beat swords into ploughshares and lances into sickles. He will change hatred into love and wrongdoing into forgiveness,' said some when they spoke of him. 'He will be a powerful king and will free us from the hands of our enemies,' said others, thinking of the hated Romans.

193

At that time there lived in the hills of Judea a priest named Zechariah. He and his wife Elizabeth were good and righteous, but they had no children. They had often asked the Lord for a son or a daughter, but now they were old and could no longer have children.

One day it was Zechariah's turn to conduct a service in the temple at Jerusalem. Zechariah dressed in his priest's robes and entered the sanctuary. In the darkened room he trembled as he looked towards the altar and saw a shining figure. It was an angel. The Lord's messenger gave out great power and strength and Zechariah was filled with dread.

The angel said, 'Fear not, Zechariah. The Lord has heard your prayer. A son will be born to you and Elizabeth. You will call him John. When he grows up, he will prepare your people for the coming of the Messiah.'

Zechariah was no longer afraid, but he was unable to believe what he had heard. If only he could have some sign to confirm the angel's words. The angel knew what Zechariah was thinking. 'I am Gabriel, the Lord's Messenger, and you do not believe me?' he said. 'You will be struck dumb from this very moment and you will not utter a word until what I have told you has come to pass.'

In front of the temple a crowd was waiting for Zechariah to give them his blessing. 'Why is he taking so long?' they asked each other in confusion. As soon as Zechariah appeared, they gathered around him, but he was only able to lift up his arms towards them. He was unable to speak, for he had received the sign that he had asked for.

Six months later the Lord sent the angel to a relative of Elizabeth's, a girl engaged to be married to Joseph, a carpenter. Her name was Mary and she lived in the village of Nazareth in Galilee. The Lord wanted to entrust Mary with a great task – she was to bring into the world the Messiah for whom people had waited so long.

'Mary,' said the Angel Gabriel, 'if you want to, you can bring to the world a great king. When he is born, you will name him Jesus, which means the Saviour, the Redeemer.'

'How can I give birth to a child? I do not even live with Joseph,' asked Mary in wonder.

'The power of the Lord will rest in you,' replied Gabriel, 'so the boy that will be born to you will be the Son of God. Your

195   *The Message of the Angel Gabriel*

relative Elizabeth is expecting a son too, even though she is so old. God can do things that human beings imagine to be impossible.'

'I shall be happy to do God's will,' said Mary. 'Let everything be as God wishes.'

As soon as Mary had spoken, the little child, the Son of God, began to grow inside her body.

Soon after this the cries of a newly born baby boy were heard in Zechariah's house.

When the neighbours heard about it, they came to see the child. 'You will name him after his father Zechariah, won't you?' they asked Elizabeth.

'No,' said Elizabeth, shaking her head. 'Our son will be called John.'

'But none of your relatives has this name, and our customs say he should be named after one of them,' argued the neighbours.

They decided to ask Zechariah. But Ze-chariah was still unable to speak. He asked the neighbours to give him a tablet, and on the tablet he wrote the words, 'His name is John.'

At that moment Zechariah recovered the power of speech. He was able to talk again and to praise the Lord. Joyfully he took the child in his arms and said, 'You, my son, will be the Lord's Prophet. You will announce the coming of the great king who will lead us to God.'

Soon these events were being talked about all over the hills of Judea and the neighbours wondered what would become of the boy whose birth had been accompanied by such omens.

Young John grew older and stronger. When he grew up he went off into the wilderness and there in the silence of the empty desert he prepared himself for the task God had given him – to tell people that the Kingdom of God was now very near.

The Message of the Angel Gabriel

How Jesus Came into the World

In Judea, not far from Jerusalem, there lies on two small hills the little town of Bethlehem, once the boyhood home of King David.

One year in winter Bethlehem was full of people. People had come from far and wide on the orders of the Roman Emperor Augustus.

Augustus ruled over a huge empire but he did not know how many subjects he had. So he issued a new proclamation. 'I have decided to count all the inhabitants of my empire so that I can levy taxes,' was the order. 'At the appointed time everyone should report to my officials in their native town and be included on the register.'

In the early evening two travellers stopped before the walls of Bethlehem – Joseph and his wife Mary of Nazareth. They had had to make the journey because Joseph came from Bethlehem, from the tribe of King David.

Mary was very tired from the journey. The child that the Angel Gabriel had foretold was soon to be born. Joseph took her to an inn and went inside to ask for lodging, but the city had many visitors, and he came out disappointed. There was no room at the inn. The exhausted travellers did not know what to do. Finally they saw an empty stable just outside the town and managed to lie down there in the hay as a long winter night settled over Bethlehem.

In the middle of that night the Son of God was born in a deserted stable. Mary wrapped the child in swaddling clothes and, because she had no cradle for him, she laid him in a wooden manger which was the feeding trough for the sheep.

The whole town was asleep except for a group of shepherds keeping watch around their fire. They could not rest as they had to watch over their flocks. Suddenly a light shone all around them and the startled shepherds saw an angel in shining clothes.

'Do not be afraid,' said the angel. 'I bring you joyous news. Today the Messiah, the Saviour of all men, has been born in Bethlehem. Go and kneel before him. It is a child in swaddling clothes lying in a manger.'

The light around the messenger of God grew brighter and brighter. More and more angels came down from Heaven to Earth and the shepherds heard them calling, 'Glory to God in Heaven, and on Earth peace to all men who love God.'

Then Bethlehem fell silent once more. The world looked as it did before, the embers glowed in the fire and high in the night sky the stars shone. Now however everything had changed. God had come down to man and given him His Son to live among men as one of them.

Great joy drove the shepherds to the stable. 'We shall surely find the child there,' they said. 'Quickly let us go to him!'

In a short while they did, indeed, find the little Jesus. He lay in the hay in the manger and slept. The shepherds gave thanks to God and told Mary and Joseph everything they had seen and heard.

Soon after this a caravan led by three men dressed in foreign clothes arrived in Jerusalem.

The men went through the narrow streets of the city and asked, 'Where is the newly born king? We saw his star in the sky. We

are sure he came to Earth in your land. We have come from far away to pay homage to him.'

News of these men soon reached the royal palace. King Herod was alarmed by the news of the newly born king. He was afraid that he had come to take his crown. He quickly summoned his learned advisers. 'Who are these strangers? Who is the king they are talking about?' he asked.

'They are Wise Men from the East, who understand the messages of the stars,' answered the advisers, 'and they are seeking the king our prophets are waiting for. He is supposed to be born in Bethlehem. It is written so in the old books: from Bethlehem a king shall come and he shall be the shepherd of the people of Israel.'

'I must get rid of this new king as quickly as possible or he could deprive me of my

power,' thought Herod. Secretly he sent a servant to summon the Wise Men and told them, 'Seek the newborn king in Bethlehem. When you find him, tell me who it is because I would also like to pay homage to him.'

It was night when the Wise Men reached Bethlehem. No light burned except the light of the stars. There among the stars the Wise Men saw the star that had led them to the land of God's people. It sparkled in the dark sky above the place where the baby Jesus slept. The Wise Men fell to the ground before the little boy. They knew that he was the Great King, even though he had no cradle. Then they opened their bags and laid their gifts on the ground. Gold, frankincense and myrrh, of the kind that burned on the altar in the Temple of God.

'Tomorrow we shall go and tell Herod that we have found the child,' decided the Wise Men, but while they slept, they

How Jesus Came into the World

heard a voice, 'Do not return to Herod because he wants to harm the child,' it warned.

The Wise Men obeyed and went home to their own country.

During the night the angel also warned Joseph, 'The child is in danger, Herod wants to find him and kill him. Get up quickly and flee to Egypt. Stay there until I speak to you again.'

Joseph woke Mary. They wrapped the baby Jesus in a cloak and before the sun was up they were already far away and safe from danger.

King Herod soon realized that the Wise Men had deceived him. In a rage he tore through the palace hurling abuse at any-one who stood in his way. Finally he summoned all his soldiers to him. 'Go to Bethlehem and kill all the baby boys up to two years old in the town and the area around it. Do not let a single one escape.'

Herod was sure that the newborn king would be among them. He thought that this cruel act would ensure a long and uninterrupted reign for him. How wrong he was! His reign did not last long and soon Herod himself died.

Then in Egypt the angel appeared once more to Joseph and said, 'Go home. Herod, who plotted to take Jesus's life, is dead.'

Joseph sat Mary and the baby Jesus on a donkey and they returned to their native land. They settled in Galilee, in the town of Nazareth. There Jesus grew up, and when he bacame a man they called him Jesus of Nazareth.

How Jesus Came into the World

In Nazareth and in the Temple

The little Jesus was like all the other boys. None of his neighbours and friends in Nazareth knew who his real father was. They thought his father was Mary's husband Joseph, who was a carpenter. Every morning, except on the day of rest, he would go off to his workshop. He made tables and ploughshares and fashioned beams. Jesus helped him in his work.

In the synagogue where the people of Nazareth praised the Lord together, there was a school. There Jesus learned to read, write and count, and, more importantly, it was there that he learned the wise words of the Old Testament and the Law of God.

At Easter Joseph and Mary went to Jerusalem. Every year crowds of pilgrims came to the festival. Even those who lived far from the holy city wanted to commemorate in the temple the Lord's freeing of His people from captivity in Egypt. When Jesus was twelve he too could go to Jerusalem.

The journey from Nazareth to Jerusalem lasted three days. Small caravans of pilgrims met other caravans and friends greeted each other and smiled as, from the hill tops, they saw for the first time the glittering white temple.

In the streets of Jerusalem the pilgrims mixed with other people. Everyone was getting ready for the celebration. In the courtyard of the temple they sacrificed a ram to the Lord and later they roasted it over a fire just as their ancestors had done before leaving Egypt. They prepared unleavened bread, wine and bitter herbs, and as night fell they sat down to a ceremonial banquet.

For a whole week the people of Jerusalem remembered how God had rescued them from slavery in Egypt and had led them back to the Promised Land. Jesus went to the temple every day. In the courtyard he saw traders selling sacrificial animals and money-changers changing

ordinary money into temple coins. People who wanted to bring a gift for the Lord tossed these temple coins into a special money-box. In the shadow of the pillars learned men taught their pupils about the Law of God, priests conducted services and people enjoyed the festive days.

When the celebrations were over, Joseph and Mary got ready to go home, but

In Nazareth and in the Temple

they could not find Jesus anywhere. People told them, 'Some of your countrymen have already left the city. Perhaps Jesus is with them.'

Joseph and Mary hurried to catch up with the pilgrims from Nazareth. They travelled for the whole day and then looked for Jesus among their friends.

'Have you seen our son?' they asked them, but no one had seen him.

With heavy hearts Joseph and Mary returned to Jerusalem. For three days they looked for Jesus all over the city. They asked people and looked for him everywhere until finally they found him in the temple. He was sitting among the learned men listening to them speak. He himself was asking and answering questions, and everyone who heard him was amazed by the wisdom of his words.

Mary ran over to Jesus. 'My son, do you not know what you have done to us? We have been looking for you everywhere. We were terribly worried about you.'

Jesus looked at his mother seriously. 'Why did you look for me? Surely you knew that I would be in my Father's house?'

Jesus was thinking of his real, heavenly Father, but neither Joseph nor Mary nor the learned men understood this.

Jesus thanked the learned men and set off on the journey home with Mary and Joseph. In Nazareth he went to the workshop with Joseph. He learned to work with a saw, an axe and a chisel. He planed planks and carried heavy beams on his shoulders. He grew strong both in body and in spirit and was dear to God and man alike.

In Nazareth and in the Temple

Jesus's Journey

One day a very special man appeared on the bank of the River Jordan. He only ate what the nearby desert provided and dressed in a rough blanket of camel hair. It was John, the son of Zechariah and Elizabeth. He told the people who passed by, 'The Kingdom of God is near. Prepare yourselves to enter it.'

'What are we supposed to do?' people wondered. 'How are we supposed to prepare ourselves?'

'Change your ways. Do not do harm to others. Give to the poor. Stop being vain,' answered John.

Those who wanted to change went into the River Jordan with John and he baptized them with water from the river. This is how he later became known as John the Baptist.

Many people wanted to see John with their own eyes. They travelled to the Jordan to see him and some were baptized. 'Are you not the Messiah that we are waiting for?' they asked, and John answered, 'No, but the Messiah will come soon.'

Crowds still flocked to the Jordan. One day a thirty-year-old man was passing and asked John to baptize him.

John gasped. 'Baptize you, Lord? I do not even deserve to undo the straps on your sandals.'

'Do as I say,' replied the man. 'I want to be with other people in everything.'

After the baptism the heavens opened and John saw the Spirit of God in the form of a dove coming down into the man.

At the time no one in the crowd knew that the newly baptized man was Jesus.

Not far from the River Jordan where John carried out his baptisms lay a barren stony wilderness. Just here and there grew tufts of yellowing grass and thorn bushes. It was to this lonely place that Jesus now went. He spoke through prayer to his Father and fasted. One day, when he was already very hungry, the Temptor, Satan, spoke to him. His voice was seductive and what he said sounded good. If the Son of God had gone along with these words, he would not have been able to lead his people to their Father in Heaven. This is what Satan wanted, but his efforts were in vain. Nothing mattered to Jesus but the will of God.

The Temptor spoke twice and twice Jesus refused him. The third time Satan took Jesus to the summit of a high mountain and showed him the world with its huge,

powerful empires, riches an glory. 'This will be your kingdom,' he said. 'I will give you all of this if you kneel before me.'

Then Jesus replied, 'Away with you, Satan. It is written in the Old Testament that one should only kneel before the Lord and worship Him alone.'

It was then that Satan realized he had lost.

Jesus remained in the wilderness for forty days. When Jesus returned from the wilderness, John was standing with two of

his disciples in the middle of the River Jordan baptizing people. When he saw Jesus, he pointed to him and said, 'Behold the Messiah. This is the Lamb of God who takes away the sins of the world.'

John's disciples, John of Zebedee and Andrew, did not wait to hear any more. They gathered up their clothes and rushed after Jesus.

'We have found the Messiah,' Andrew said later to his brother Simon the Fisherman, who had also come down to the River Jordan. 'We spoke to him. Come, let me take you to him.'

This is how Jesus came to know Andrew, Simon and John, the young son of the fisherman Zebedee.

The next day Jesus decided to return to Galilee. On the way he stopped in towns and villages and everywhere he went he told the people about the Kingdom of God. 'Now it is like a little seed,' he told them, 'but from this little seed a mighty tree will grow. Just as the birds fly to the crown of a mighty tree and build safe nests in its branches, so people from far and wide will find their true home in the Kingdom of God.'

Soon all the people who had previously travelled to see John at the River of Jordan wanted to see and hear Jesus. On one occasion on the shores of Lake Galilee, so many people were pushing and shoving around him that he had nowhere to go. In front of him was the mass of people and behind him was the lake, but two little

209

boats rocked gently on the shallow water. Some fishermen stood in them pulling in their nets. Jesus saw that one of them was Simon. 'Could you lend me your boat?' he asked.

Simon drew up close to the shore and Jesus spoke to the crowd from the boat.

At noon the crowd dispersed and Jesus said, 'Simon, I want to thank you for your help. Go back out on to the lake and cast your net.'

'But we will not catch anything, Master,' objected Simon. 'We tried all night. However, we will do as you say.'

The fishermen sailed off into the middle of the lake and then they could scarcely believe their eyes. They had hardly cast their nets than they had to ask another boat to help them land their catch. Shining silvery fish were everywhere – on the sand, in the boats, in the nets. Simon had never seen so many. He remembered what Andrew had said to him about Jesus and he fell to his knees before him in distress. 'Lord, please leave me,' he said in fear. 'You are great and powerful and I am just a sinful mortal.'

Jesus smiled at him. 'Do not be afraid and come with me. You will no longer have to wory about fish, but about people.'

So Simon stood up and left his boat, his net and his catch on the shore and followed Jesus.

Not far from there in the village of Cana there was a wedding. All their neighbours and friends came to congratulate the newly-weds. Jesus was there too with his first disciples and his mother Mary. Toasts were drunk and the guests sang songs and made merry, but the bride and groom soon becamc sad. Mary noticed this. She leaned over to Jesus and whispered, 'Son, they are poor and they do not have enough wine for their guests. That is why they are upset.'

'Do not worry,' replied Jesus softly, 'I know about this.'

Mary slipped away unnoticed and went to the people who were handing out the drinks. 'Do everything my son tells you,' she said.

Six large stone pitchers stood by one of the walls in the house. Jesus pointed to them and said, 'Fill them to the brim with water. Then pour some into the cup and give it to the governor of this feast.'

He had hardly taken his first sip when his eyes began to shine. 'This is wonderful wine,' he said happily, calling the bridegroom to him. 'People usually serve the best wine first at feasts and keep the bad wine for later, but you have kept the best wine for now,' he said happily.

Jesus's disciples knew where the good wine had come from and they were now

Jesus's Journey

sure that their Master was not an ordinary man.

Jesus did not remain long in Cana. Once again he journeyed to the towns and small villages and told the people that God loved them. Often sick people came to him and he healed them. He gave sight to the blind, and hearing to the deaf, and the crippled were able to run and jump again. As he travelled he gathered more an more disciples around him and from them he chose twelve men, who were later called his apostles. They were to accompany Jesus everywhere and to remember everything he did and said, so that when the time came they could tell other people. Simon the Fisherman was one of the twelve. Simon often spoke for the other eleven and was able to make decisions when others were not able. Jesus gave him a new name, Peter, which means the Rock, and this made Simon very happy. All of them loved Jesus – Simon Peter and his brother Andrew, the brothers James and John Zebedee, Philip and his friend Bartholomew, Thomas and Matthew, James the son of Alphaeus, Judas the son of James and Simon called Zelotes.

The twelfth, Judas Iscariot, was different from the others. He thought that the Kingdom of God, which Jesus spoke about so often, would bring him wealth. For Judas loved money.

Just before the time we call Easter, the twelve apostles went with Jesus to Jerusalem. They marvelled at the mighty colonnades in the temple, but Jesus took no notice of the building. He stood in the temple courtyard and watched. All around him people were buying and selling livestock, traders were bartering, money-changers were counting their money to see how much they had earned from changing ordinary money into temple coins. All around was noise and confusion. Jesus became angry. He fashioned a whip from some strands of rope and began to crack it. At once the traders, cattle and sheep ran from the temple. The money-changers crawled about next to their overturned tables to find their money. Jesus said to the dove-sellers, 'Take these things away from here! Do not make my Father's house into a marketplace. This is a house of prayer.'

The learned men saw this confusion from behind the colonnade. 'Who is this man who dares to destroy the established order?' they asked in outrage. 'We must be careful of this man.'

After the festival, Jesus set off on another journey. Sometimes people invited him to spend the night in their homes, on other occasions he slept beneath the trees covered by a blanket. He only had to stop somewhere and a crowd would gather round him. Jesus would say to them, 'Do not be so concerned with your own life, about what you eat and drink and wear. Seek the Kingdom of God and His righteousness and God will give you what you need.'

'But what is the righteousness of the Kingdom of God?' people asked.

'Do unto others as they do unto you. Do

not condemn others and God will not condemn you. Forgive others and God will forgive you. Give to others and God will give to you. Evil shall be repaid with evil.'

Then Jesus said something that people did not understand at all. 'Love your enemies and you will be the sons of God, for He lets the Sun shine on both good and evil and brings the rain to both the righteous and the unrighteous.'

'But it is difficult to love one's enemies,' said people shrugging their shoulders.

'Of course,' said Jesus. 'The road of destruction is wide and the gate is large, but

213

the road to the Kingdom of God is narrow and the gate is small. I will help you to travel along this difficult road.'

On one occasion when Jesus had healed many sick people and had spoken for a long time about the Kingdom of God, he and his disciples wanted to sail across to the other side of Lake Galilee. He was very tired that day. As soon as the boat pulled away from the shore, he lay down and fell asleep. The disciples became worried when they looked at the sky. Dark storm clouds were gathering. Lake Galilee is so large that it was called a sea, and in a storm the small fishing boat could easily sink. The disciples began rowing but the shore was a long way off. Suddenly a gale blew up. The wind whipped up the surface of the water and the waves began to crash over the boat.

'We are sinking!' cried the disciples in alarm. 'We cannot keep the water out.'

The storm got worse but Jesus slept on peacefully. As a huge wave approached, the disciples cried, 'Master, we are going to die!'

Jesus opened his eyes, stood up and stretched out his arms to the wind and the waves. At that moment the lake became calm and a gentle breeze blew over the surface of the water. 'Why were you so worried?' asked Jesus. 'Do you not have faith in my power?'

Long afterwards the disciples still talked

about the fact that even the wind obeyed their Master.

The whole country soon knew about Jesus's miracles. Wherever he went, people welcomed him. On the road to the town of Jericho, a large crowd had gathered. Among them was a little man. He stood on tip-toe and peered over the shoulders of others, but still he could not see Jesus. This little man was an official called Zacchaeus. Everyone held Zacchaeus in contempt. He collected taxes and duties for the hated Romans and often cheated people out of money so that he could keep it for himself. In this way, Zacchaeus became very rich, but now he no longer thought of money. He only wanted to belong to Jesus. A little way from the road there was a sycamore tree and Zacchaeus had an idea. He ran over to the tree and climbed up to its branches. There he had a fine view. It did not matter to him that his fine clothes were torn and dirty and the people were laughing at him. He sat on a branch and looked out for Jesus.

Soon after this Jesus came up to the tree. 'Zacchaeus,' he said, 'come down. I want to stay in your house today.'

Zacchaeus's face flushed with delight. He quickly climbed down and took Jesus and his disciples to his house.

'He wants to be the guest of a criminal,' grumbled some of the onlookers. There were some learned men among them and they spoke to the disciples. 'Does your Master not know that it is not right to mix with people like Zacchaeus?' they asked sternly.

Zacchaeus, however, was happy. He had a beautiful, richly furnished house, but no one ever came to visit him. Now he had Jesus as a guest. When he entered his house, however, he hung his head. All at once he felt ashamed of his beautiful house and his ill-gotten possessions. 'Lord,' he blurted out, 'I will give half my goods to the poor, and if I have cheated anyone I will repay him four times over.'

On that day Zacchaeus changed completely. He became a new, happier man.

Jesus continued to travel the roads of his native land. He told the people about the Kingdom of God and brought them joy. He did not allow himself any rest even when he was very tired. He knew he had enemies and that his time was short.

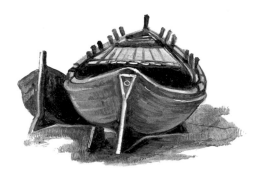

Jesus's Journey

The Good Samaritan and the Prodigal Son

Jesus travelled from town to town, from village to village. He spoke on the shores of Lake Galilee, in the mountains and in the synagogues, and in all these places people listened attentively to him. Among them were scribes and Pharisees, learned men, who studied the law of God and taught people how to behave if they were to do as God wished.

On one occasion the learned men asked Jesus, 'Master, which of the Ten Commandments is the most important?'

Jesus replied, 'Love God above all things and love your neighbour as you love yourself.'

'But what does it mean to love our neighbour,' they asked.

Jesus replied with a parable, 'A man was walking from Jerusalem to Jericho when he was attacked by robbers on a dangerous part of the road. They robbed him, beat him and threw him into the bushes. Then a priest came. He saw the injured man but pretended that he had not seen him and continued his journey. Soon afterwards a temple servant hurried by. He too saw the unfortunate man but did not stop. Then a stranger, a Samaritan came along the road. As soon as he saw the injured man, he rushed over to him. He tended the man's wounds, put him on his mule and took him to an inn, where he looked after him. The next day he gave some money to the innkeeper and said, "Please look after this man. If it costs more than this, I will pay you when I come back this way." '

Jesus then asked one of the scribes, 'Which of these three loved his neighbour?'

'The one who helped the injured man,' replied one of the scribes.

'Then go and do as the Samaritan did,' said Jesus.

Officials like Zacchaeus and other people whom others wanted nothing to do with often came to see Jesus. The scribes and Pharisees did not like this. 'These people do not uphold the Law of God. They are sinners,' they said to the disciples. 'Why does the Master associate with them? Why does he eat and drink with them?'

Jesus heard this and said, 'What does the shepherd do if he has a hundred sheep and one of them gets lost? He leaves the ninety-nine in a safe place and goes to look for the one that has got lost. Then when he finds it, he puts it on his shoulders and carries it joyfully home. The people you are talking about are like lost sheep, and I am a good shepherd. I look after all my sheep. I know them by name and when I call them they hear me and come to me. I came into this world so that none of them would get lost and die. I would give my own life for them.' Then he told them a tale of love and forgiveness.

'A man had two sons. The younger one said to his father, "Give me what is mine.

I want to go out into the world and use my life." When he had received his share from his father, he sold it and with the money went off to a distant land. There he lived a life of pleasure until he had spent all his money. At the time there was a great famine in that land and he did not even have a crust of bread to eat. He had to look after pigs, and would have liked to eat the peelings the pigs ate but he did not even get these. "Even the labourers have enough bread to eat," he thought, "but I am hungry. I shall go back home." Feeling sorry for wasting his money, he set off. He was still far from home when his father caught sight of him and rushed to welcome him. The son said, "Father, I no longer deserve to be your son, but please take me as one of your labourers." However, his father called the servants and said, "Bring some fine clothes for my son. Give him some new sandals and a ring for his finger. Kill the fatted calf and let us have feast."

The elder son was working in the fields. When he came home, he heard music coming from the house. He asked a servant what was going on and the servant replied, "Your brother has come home and your father is happy that he is home again." The elder brother was angry and did not want to go inside. His father came out and spoke to him, but the elder son became even angrier. "I have served you for all these years and have always done what you have told me," he shouted. "In all this time you have never even given me a kid to roast so I could enjoy myself with my friends. Now, as soon as your prodigal son returns, you order a calf to be killed for him." His father replied, "Son, you are always with me and everything I have is yours, but we have a reason to celebrate because your brother was dead and now he is alive again. He was lost and now he is found."'

Jesus had spoken but the learned men grew angry. They did not want to believe him. Their ill-feelings towards Jesus grew and grew. They followed him around and watched his words and deeds.

Jesus Heals

On his travels Jesus often visited the little town of Capernaum, which lay not far from Lake Galilee. In Capernaum his disciples Peter and Andrew had a small house, with a flat roof which could be reached by an outer flight of outside steps. Jesus sometimes spent time up on the roof.

When the people of Capernaum heard

that Jesus was coming, so many people gathered around the house that it was impossible to move in front of the door. Everybody wanted to see and hear him or ask him for help.

Then four men pushed their way through the throng with a stretcher. On it lay a paralysed man who was unable to walk. They thought that Jesus could help

him, but did not know how to get through the crowd so that they might reach Jesus. Finally they carried the paralysed man on to the roof, pulled up the mat that covered it and lowered him down through the opening to Jesus. When Jesus saw the faith that the men had in him, he said to the paralysed man, 'Do not be sad. All your sins are pardoned.'

A number of Pharisees sat among the other guests in the house. 'What is the man saying?' they thought. 'Now he is blaspheming. Only God can pardon sins.'

Jesus knew what the Pharisees were thinking. 'To show you that I have the power to pardon sins, I shall give you a sign,' he said. He turned to the paralysed man and said, 'Stand up. Take your blanket and go home.'

The man leapt up and joyfully returned to his family.

Soon after this a man called Jairus ran to Jesus. He was one of the elders of the synagogue.

'Please come with me,' he begged Jesus. 'My daughter is sick at home and I am afraid she is going to die.'

Jairus looked very worried. He was afraid that Jesus would not get there in time. And they had only gone a couple of yards when a man came running up. 'Do not trouble the Master any more,' he told Jairus sadly. 'Your daughter is already dead.'

Jairus went pale with grief, but Jesus comforted him, 'Jairus, do not be afraid. Just have faith in me.'

Jesus Heals

They both entered the house. The room was already full of friends and relatives lamenting over the dead girl.

'Please leave and do not weep,' said Jesus. 'The girl is not dead. She is asleep.'

'Are you blind?' they scoffed. 'Anyone can see she is dead.'

Then Jesus went over to the girl and took her cold hand. 'Get up,' he said.

The girl opened her eyes and jumped up from the bed. Everyone saw it and was astonished. Then Jesus said, 'Bring the girl something to eat. She is hungry.'

On days of rest Jesus would go to the synagogue and tell the whole congregation about his Father. There too sick people would come to him. The Pharisees did not like this. 'There are six days for work,'

they told the sick. 'You should come on those days to be healed and not on the day of rest, because this is forbidden by our scriptures.'

Among themselves they said, 'This man deliberately heals the sick on the Lord's day. He wants to show us that he is bringing the Kingdom of God to the Earth and that he is the promised Messiah. How can the son of a carpenter from Nazareth be a Messiah?'

Others replied, 'He *is* the Messiah. His words have power. Could anyone else produce greater marvels than him?'

Even these wonderful miracles of Jesus did not convince the learned men. They had their own secret thoughts about him and would tell no one.

Jesus Heals

The Miracles of Jesus

Everyone knew the name of Jesus of Nazareth. Shepherds, fishermen, craftsmen and other people burdened by everyday worries, came in large numbers to the Master of Nazareth. On one occasion there were about five thousand of them on the shores of Lake Galilee. Jesus spoke for a long time about the Kingdom of God and healed the sick. People did not realize how late it had become.

Before the Sun set, Jesus asked a disci-

ple, 'How much food do we have with us? All these people are hungry.'

'We have just five loaves and two fishes,' replied Andrew.

'Bring them to me,' Jesus said, 'and tell the people to sit on the grass.'

When all the people were comfortably seated, Jesus took the bread and the fishes, gave thanks to God and began to break them. He gave the pieces to his disciples and they took them to the crowd. Each person got as much as they wanted until everyone was full, and still twelve pieces were left over.

Then the crowd began to rejoice. 'He is the one we have been waiting for. Let us proclaim him King!'

Now Jesus had not come into the world to become an earthly king. He made his disciples get into the boat and sail away while he hid in the hills.

It was nearly morning but the disciples were still on the lake. A strong wind was blowing against their boat. At daybreak

The Miracles of Jesus

they looked around. They saw the dark waves and, in the distance they could just make out the shoreline. Then suddenly they saw an amazing sight. A figure was approaching on the surface of the water. 'A phantom, a phantom!' they cried in fear.

'Do not be alarmed. It is me,' came a voice which the disciples realized was that of Jesus.

'Lord, if that really is you, just tell me and I will come to you over the water,' said Peter.

'Come,' said Jesus.

Peter climbed over the side of the boat and looked across to Jesus. He took one step, then another, then a third. He really was walking on the water as if it was solid ground. Then the wind whipped up a large wave and Peter became afraid. 'What if I sink?' he thought. Hardly had he thought it than the surface of the water opened up beneath him and Peter plunged into the depths.

'Lord, save me,' he cried. Jesus caught Peter and pulled him out of the water. 'Peter, why did you doubt me?' he said.

Jesus and his drenched disciple climbed into the boat and soon they reached the shore.

The people whom Jesus had fed the previous evening on the five loaves and two fishes remained on the other side of the lake. They knew that the Master had not sailed away with his disciples and in the morning they searched for him everywhere. They wanted him to give them

something for breakfast, but could not see him anywhere. When they realized that he was not there, they got into a boat and began to look for him. Soon afterwards they found him, but he did not welcome them in quite the way they expected.

'You only think of filling your stomachs,' he said, 'and you do not try to find the food that will give you eternal life.'

'What kind of food is that, Master?' they asked him.

'It is me,' replied Jesus. 'I am the living bread that God has sent you. My body and my blood are the true food of life.'

These words caused some disbelief. 'How can his body be food? This is nonsense.' Shocked, they turned away from Jesus and said, 'We will no longer listen to him.'

On that day many of the people who had gone with Jesus from place to place left him. Jesus watched them leave and then turned to his twelve disciples and asked, 'Do you want to go too?'

'Who would we go to, Lord?' replied Peter. 'You know we have always believed that you were sent by God.'

'One of you does not believe,' said Jesus softly, 'and the hour is now near when I shall be betrayed to the hands of my enemies.'

There was at that time in Jerusalem a young man who had been born blind. He had never seen light, people or trees. He sat on the ground and begged for money. He was doing this when Jesus saw him.

Jesus anointed his eyes with mud and

The Miracles of Jesus

226

said, 'Now go and wash in the pool.'

The young man obeyed and suddenly he could see. How beautiful the world was!

It was the seventh day of the week, the day of rest.

Many Pharisees lived in Jerusalem and they were quick to hear of everything. They summoned the young man to them. 'Do you know that the man who opened your eyes is a sinner?' they said. 'According to our scriptures, such things may not be done on the day of rest. Anyone who breaks the laws of the holy day has sinned.'

'But that is very strange,' replied the young man. 'You say yourselves that God does not listen to sinners but listens to those who do His will. If that man had not been sent by God, he would not have been able to give me the gift of sight.'

The Pharisees rounded on the young man. 'You fool! You are a sinner and you are trying to lecture us? Away with you!'

Jesus saw the young man the Pharisees

The Miracles of Jesus

had thrown out and asked him, 'Do you believe in the Messiah?'

'Who is he, if I am to believe in him?' replied the young man.

'He is standing before you,' said Jesus. 'He opened your eyes.'

'I believe, Master,' cried the young man and fell to his knees.

Jesus turned to the bystanders and said, 'I am the light of the world. Whosoever goes with me will not grope in the darkness but will have the light of life.'

Later Jesus was walking in the temple by the pillars of Solomon. The Pharisees saw him and immediately surrounded him. 'How long are you going to keep us in this state of uncertainty?' they asked. 'Are you the Messiah? Tell us openly.'

'I am constantly telling you but you do not believe me,' replied Jesus. 'If you do not believe my words, at least believe the deeds I am doing in the name of my Father. Such deeds should have long since convinced you. I and the Father are one and the same.'

'He is blaspheming!' cried the Pharisees. 'He is a man and he claims to be equal to God!'

In their anger they set upon him and tried to stone him, but they did not manage to get their hands on him. Jesus slipped away and left the city.

Jesus left Judea with his disciples and stayed for a while in a remote place. There he heard some sad news. His friend Lazarus had fallen seriously ill. He was given this news by Lazarus's sisters Mary and Martha. They both begged him to come and heal Lazarus. Jesus was very fond of Martha, Mary and Lazarus. They lived in Judea, in the village of Bethany not far from Jerusalem, and Jesus often visited them when he was on his travels.

'Let us return to Judea,' Jesus said to his disciples. 'Lazarus is asleep, but I shall wake him.'

'Lord, not long ago they tried to stone you in Judea and now you want to go back there?' the disciples protested. 'If Lazarus is asleep, he will recover. Sleep gives strength to the sick.'

Jesus shook his head. 'You do not understand me. Lazarus has just died. Let us go to him.'

Meanwhile a crowd of people had gathered in Bethany. Everyone in Jerusalem knew Lazarus and his sisters and now they had all come to comfort Mary and Martha in their grief. One of them saw Jesus coming and told Martha.

Martha came out to meet Jesus. 'Master, if you had been here, my brother would not have died,' she said sorrowfully.

'Lazarus will rise up,' replied Jesus. 'I am the resurrection and the life for all who believe in me.'

Martha told her sister about Jesus's arrival. Mary dried the tears from her eyes and quickly stood up. Her friends thought she was going to Lazarus's tomb to mourn there and ran after her. They saw her lying in her grief at Jesus's feet. Jesus had tears in his eyes. Softly he asked her, 'Where have you buried him?'

Mary and Martha led Jesus to the tomb. It was a cave, the entrance of which was covered by a large rock.

'Move that stone,' said Jesus.

'Master, do not go in there,' said Martha in horror. 'He died four days ago, you know.'

'Martha, have you already forgotten what I said to you a few moments ago?' replied Jesus.

Several men were needed to move the heavy rock. They were surprised by the request but obeyed nonetheless and then looked expectantly at Jesus. No one moved or said a word.

Jesus called into the deep silence of the tomb, 'Lazarus, come out!'

Then they all shouted in terror. Lazarus appeared at the mouth of the cave. His arms and legs were wrapped in the funeral shroud, so Jesus said, 'Unbind him so he may go home.'

Martha, Mary and the funeral guests were overjoyed that Lazarus had risen from the grave, but there were people in Bethany who went straight to Jerusalem to tell the Pharisees what Jesus had done now.

There was turmoil among the scribes and Pharisees. They immediately summoned a council of the elders and priests of Jerusalem.

'He is leading people away from the Law,' shouted some of those in the council. Others said, 'We cannot deny that he performs great miracles. If we let things remain this way then everyone will believe in him. People are following him and are not coming to the temple and paying their temple dues.'

'You do not understand anything,' yelled a man who particularly hated Jesus. This was the high priest Caiaphas. 'That rabble might proclaim him king and the Romans would not like that. Our land is full of their soldiers. They will attack us and destroy our temple, our city, our whole nation.'

Then the decision was taken: Jesus of Nazareth must die.

The Miracles of Jesus

Judas's Betrayal

Almost three years had passed since the wedding in Cana, where Jesus had turned the water into wine, and now again the Easter celebrations were drawing near. This time too, caravans of pilgrims headed for Jerusalem for the festivities. There were so many people that they could not all get into the city. Some camped in tents below the city walls and others found places to stay in the surrounding villages.

In Jerusalem and in the pilgrims' tents all the talk was about Lazarus. 'Have you heard about Jesus's miracle in Bethany?' people asked. 'Lazarus had been in his grave for four days and Jesus brought him back to life. I hope we see the Master of Nazareth with our own eyes during the festival.'

'He probably is not coming this year,' said some, expressing their doubts. 'You know that the high priest wants him arrested.'

Jesus and his disciples approached Jerusalem from the city of Jericho. The air was fresh and fragrant and flowers bloomed in the valleys, but the disciples trudged along behind Jesus. Lately he had often spoken to them about his death. 'It must be so,' he comforted them. 'A grain of wheat once sown in the earth also must die so that it can grow into a new ear of wheat and I will rise from the dead on the third day.' Yet his words only raised their spirits briefly.

At a crossroads near Jerusalem, Jesus sent two of his disciples for a young donkey. When they brought it, they put a cloak on its back and Jesus sat on it.

The rider was soon spotted by the people who had their tents outside the walls of Jerusalem. 'It is Jesus, the Master of Nazareth,' they cried to the other pilgrims. 'He is arriving like a king. It was written so in the scriptures: "The king will arrive in silence, sitting on a donkey."'

People rushed towards the road from all sides. 'Hosanna, Hosanna!' they cried joyously, waving green branches at Jesus by way of greeting and placing their cloaks in the dust in front of the donkey. Jesus rode on them, as if on a coloured carpet, all the way to the gates of the temple.

Jesus's disciples were delighted by this welcome. All at once the worry they felt for their Master's life left them. It was only those who were nearest to Jesus who heard him speaking to God: 'Father, I am filled with worry. Yet what can I say? Save me from my hour of suffering? But it was for this hour that I came into the world.

Well, let it be according to your will.' In the temple courtyard people had gathered from all over the city. 'Hosanna!' they cried when Jesus spoke.

'Do you hear that?' the high priests said to one another. They stood in a huddle some way off, their faces purple with anger. 'Even some of the Pharisees are praising him. We must get rid of him as soon as possible.'

'But how?' asked some. 'It is not possible in public. They are all behind him. The people would rise up against us.'

'We will wait until he is alone in some quiet corner,' they decided.

The Easter celebrations were due to start in a few days timc. Jesus spent all his time in the temple healing the sick and speaking to people about his Father. At

231

Judas's Betrayal

night he went outside the city and slept in the Garden of Gethsemane on the nearby Mount of Olives.

One day Jesus stopped on the hillside on his way from the temple and looked back across the valley. Before him lay the city, brown and white in the twilight, with the wonderful temple at its centre.

'Look how beautiful the temple is, Master,' said one of the disciples.

Jesus turned to his disciple with a serious expression on his face. 'Do you admire that great building? Not a stone of it will remain in place.'

The disciples were sad. 'But surely that will happen at the end of the world, at the end of time?' they said softly.

'It will happen much, much earlier.'

'And when will the end of the world be?' asked the disciples.

'No one knows the day and the hour of the end of the world,' replied Jesus. 'The angels in Heaven do not know and neither do I. Only my Father knows; but then I will come into the world again, surrounded in glory and accompanied by angels. I will sit on the throne and all nations will gather before me, all the people that have lived on Earth since the world began, and I will divide them one from the other. To those on my right I will say, "Come, you righteous ones, and take the kingdom that awaits you. When I was hungry, you gave me food. When I was thirsty, you gave me water. When I was travelling, you took me in. When I was naked, you clothed me. When I was sick, you came to see me and when I was in prison, you came there too." And the righteous will ask, "Lord, when did we do this for you? We have never met you." And I will say to them, "What you have done for one man you have done for me." But to those on my left I will say, "Go away from me. There is no place for you in the kingdom because you have done none of this for me." And they will protest, "How could we, when we have never seen you hungry, thirsty, tired from

travelling, naked, ill or in prison." And I will answer them, "What you have never done for one man who needed your help you have not done for me."'

The disciples did not know whether to rejoice at the thought of Jesus's second coming, or to be sad at the sight of his serious expression. They lay beneath the low branches of the olive trees and did not even notice that Judas was not there with them.

Judas had left the others when they were coming out of the temple. He wondered how much the high priests would pay him if he told them where to find Jesus. He knew very well that they wanted to get rid of Jesus because the whole city was talking about it.

Judas waited until the others were out of sight and then he went to see the high priest Caiaphas. 'What would you give me to betray Jesus of Nazareth?' he asked.

Caiaphas soon agreed to pay Judas thirty silver dinars. Judas was happy with the price. He could buy a slave for that sort of money.

Soon after this, Jesus sent two of his disciples to the home of one of his friends in Jerusalem. 'He will take you to the upstairs room,' he said, 'and there you will prepare the Easter lamb.'

In the evening Jesus and the other disciples came to the house. In the entrance hall they could already smell the roast lamb. In the middle of the table was a dish of sauce, there was wine, unleavened bread and bitter herbs, whose taste was supposed to remind them of the suffering of the captivity in Egypt. The Easter feast could now begin. The disciples waited for Jesus to take the seat of honour at the head of the table, but their Master did something that surprised them. He took off his cloak, wrapped himself in linen and went to each of his disciples in turn with a bowl of water and washed their feet.

'Do you understand what I have done?' asked Jesus, when he had dressed again.

The puzzled disciples simply shook their puzzled heads. Washing feet was servant's work. Why did their Lord and Master demean himself so?

'I would like you to follow my example,' said Jesus, 'and for you to render the others the kind of service that I have just rendered to you. Love as I loved you.'

The disciples lowered their eyes. Jesus seemed to be saying goodbye to them. John sighed and sorrowfully laid his head on Jesus's shoulder.

'I have been looking forward to eating this lamb with you before I suffer,' said Jesus. Then he said, 'One of you will betray me.'

The disciples were shocked. This was impossible, they thought, as they looked at one another in alarm, but they knew that their Master never uttered empty words. 'Perhaps will I betray you, Lord?' they asked in turn.

Judas also looked up from the table. 'Perhaps am I the betrayer?' he asked, not even blushing.

John leaned over to Jesus and whis-

pered, 'Tell me who it is that will betray you.'

'The one I am breaking this bread for,' whispered Jesus, dipping the bread into the dish and giving it to Judas. 'Do what you are going to do now,' he told him.

Without a word, Judas stood up, opened the door and went out into the darkness. The others imagined that he was going off to do something important and Jesus did not say anything to them. He took some bread and, after thanking his Father for it, he began to break it and give it to his disciples.

'Take it and eat,' he told them, 'and when I have left you, break the bread in this way. This bread is my body which I give to you.'

After supper, he took a cup of wine and gave it to the disciples. Each one drank from it. 'This chalice is my blood which I shed for you and for all mankind. With this I countenance a new contract which shall remain with man for all time.'

The disciples remembered that Jesus had spoken about his body and blood once before. Then he had said it was the food of life, but this thought did not comfort the disciples.

They were still sad. They felt that something bad would happen that night. Peter hid a sword beneath his cloak.

After the supper, they returned from the city to the Mount of Olives. On the way, Jesus looked at his group of friends and said, 'Tonight you will all forsake me.'

Peter furtively touched his hidden sword. 'Even if they all forsake you, I will never forsake you!' he cried.

'Peter,' replied Jesus softly, 'before the cock crows, you will deny me three times.'

In the Garden of Gethsemane, the disciples spread their cloaks on the grass and prepared to go to sleep. Then Jesus turned to Peter, James and John and said, 'Stay awake with me. I am sorrowful, even unto death.'

Then he went a few steps away from them and fell to his knees in anguish. 'Father,' he prayed, 'if it is possible, let my suffering pass in the next few hours.' After a while he got up and went to the three disciples. He found them asleep. 'Peter, can you not watch over me for just one hour,' he said sadly. He went away for a second time and whispered, 'Father, cannot my suffering pass and can I pass through it so that your will may be done.'

The disciples had fallen asleep once more. This time Jesus did not wake them. He prayed until the silence of the night was disturbed by the sound of footsteps. An armed column was making its way up the side of the Mount of Olives, swords clattering and glinting in the light of torches. At its head was Judas.

Judas's Betrayal

The Death of Jesus

I t was the middle of the night in Jerusalem and all was dark. Except, that is, on the slopes of the Mount of Olives where the light of torches could be seen flashing. This light woke the disciples. 'Get up,' said Jesus. 'My betrayer is approaching.'

The disciples rubbed their eyes and were startled to see the armed column. Suddenly they saw Judas.

Judas had everything well thought out. On the way there he had made a plan with the temple guard. 'It will be dark in the garden and everything will be confused. You must act quickly and arrest the right man. Take the man I greet with a kiss.'

Then Judas pressed his lips to Jesus's cheek. 'Greetings, Master,' he said.

'My friend, do you betray me with a kiss?' whispered Jesus. Then he turned to the people armed with swords and staves and said, 'Who are you seeking?'

'Jesus of Nazareth,' they replied.

'That is me,' said Jesus.

No sooner had the people heard his voice than they stepped back and fell to the ground.

'Who are you seeking?' asked Jesus again.

Then the disciples came to their senses. Peter remembered his sword. He drew it and cut off the right ear of the nearest attacker.

'Put away your sword,' Jesus told Peter. 'I must suffer my fate.' Then he touched the wounded man and all traces of his injury disappeared.

'This is your hour and the kingdom of darkness,' said Jesus to the armed men. 'If it is me you seek, then let the others go.'

The attackers rallied. They twisted Jesus's arms and tied them behind his back. In no time at all they had taken him down to Jerusalem.

The armed men took their prisoner to Annas, a former high priest.

Then Caiaphas prepared to have Jesus tried.

He sent a servant to the city to wake the members of the Grand Council and to summon them to a special night session. One by one the priests, scribes and elders assembled in Caiaphas's house. They already knew what the verdict would be. They only hoped that the meeting would be over quickly before the news of Jesus's arrest could spread through the city. False witnesses were prepared. They had to claim before the Grand Council that Jesus

had done something that warranted the death penalty.

The meeting did not pass quickly, however. The testimonies of the witnesses did not tally and Jesus did not answer any questions. Caiaphas flushed red with anger. No charge had yet been proved and if things went on like this, Jesus would have to be released. Caiaphas decided on one last step. He stood up and, with all the dignity of a high priest, stood before Jesus. 'I challenge you to swear by the Living God whether you are the Messiah and the Son of the Lord on High.'

The Council fell silent. What would Jesus say? Would he say that he was not the Messiah and thereby save his life. Then he would be no longer dangerous. His followers would desert him and everything would be as it was before.

'I am exactly as you have said,' replied Jesus, 'and soon you will see me surrounded by the glory of the Lord on High.'

'He has blasphemed! He has blasphemed!' cried Caiaphas. 'You all heard him. We do not need any witnesses now. This man has condemned himself.'

His servants seized Jesus. They dragged him down the corridor into the yard and beat him. Blood soon ran down Jesus's face.

The disciples Peter and John did not want to desert their Master. When the armed men took Jesus out of the garden, they followed at a distance. In the city, they summoned the courage to enter the courtyard of the high priest's house through a side entrance.

The guard at the gate looked into Peter's face. 'Are you not a disciple of that man from Galilee?' he asked.

'No, no,' said Peter, shaking his head and hurrying past into the courtyard.

It was a cold night. The servants and armed men stood around the fire they had made in the courtyard. Behind them the guard stood watch over Jesus. Peter also went up to the fire and warmed his hands. Then over the heads of the servants he caught sight of his Master. Among so many enemies he felt afraid. When the light of the fire lit up Peter's face, one of the armed men drew his sword. 'You are a disciple of that man from Nazareth!' he cried. 'I saw you with him in the garden.'

'Where do you get that idea from?' said Peter, turning pale. 'I have never even met him.'

'What do you mean?' someone said. 'You are from Galilee, just like he is.'

'I do not know what you are talking about,' blurted Peter. 'I do not know him.'

At that moment a cock crowed somewhere. Jesus turned and looked at Peter. Peter fled from the courtyard and wept bitter tears.

The Sun had hardly risen when the Grand Council pronounced its verdict: Jesus of Nazareth was sentenced to death. The high priests, their servants and the temple guard took Jesus off in chains to their ruler. This was the Roman, Pontius Pilate, who was the Roman Emperor's representative in Jerusalem. Pilate was supposed to confirm the sentence of the Grand Council. 'Before the people of Jerusalem wake to a new day,' thought Caiaphas, 'Jesus will be in the hands of the Romans and then no one will be able to save him.'

Pilate came out into the courtyard of his palace and cast his eyes over the crowd. 'What is this man accused of?' he asked.

'Of inciting the whole nation to rebellion,' they replied and added, 'He claims to be King of the Jews.'

Pilate went back into his palace and sent some soldiers to bring Jesus to him. 'Are you the King of the Jews?' he asked him.

'I am a king,' replied Jesus, 'but my kingdom is not of this world. If it were I would have my own soldiers, and they

The Death of Jesus

would fight to keep me from falling into the hands of my enemies.'

Pilate did not understand this answer. He had never heard of the Kingdom of God, and so he could not understand what Jesus was saying. He wondered how a king without soldiers could be dangerous and went back out into the courtyard and said to the high priests, 'That man has done nothing that deserves the death penalty. It is the custom that at Easter I release one prisoner. So this time I shall release your king.'

'No! Not that!' they cried. 'Release another prisoner. Release the insurgent, Barabbas.'

Pilate frowned. 'I shall punish the man from Nazareth and then I shall release him.'

The punishment Pilate decided on was a lashing. The Romans called lashing 'little death' and, indeed, some prisoners did die from it.

Pilate ordered his soldiers to take a whip and carry out the sentence.

'The Jews have a fine king,' they laughed. They threw a purple cloak over his lacerated back and put a crown of thorns on his head. 'Hail, King of the Jews,' they shouted, bowing to him mockingly.

Jesus could hardly stand. He was covered in blood and his swollen face was barely recognizable. When Pilate brought him out again, the people in the courtyard looked away. 'Crucify him! Crucify him!'

they cried. 'He must die because he pretended to be the Son of God!'

Pilate was alarmed. He would have preferred to release Jesus. Once again he turned to the high priests and said, 'Do you want me to crucify your king?'

'We do not have a king. We have a Roman Emperor,' cried Caiaphas, 'and anyone who proclaims himself king is the Emperor's enemy. If you release Jesus of Nazareth, you will show that you too are the Emperor's enemy!'

Pilate was afraid. The suspicious Emperor might believe such an accusation. He would send Pilate into exile or worse. He was reluctant to take matters any further. He confirmed the sentence and gave Jesus to the soldiers, who led him off to his death.

A sad procession came out of Jerusalem. In front and behind went Roman soldiers. In the middle staggered Jesus. On his back he carried a heavy beam. A slow, cruel death on the cross awaited him.

At the place called Golgotha, meaning *skull,* the procession halted. There bare posts stood stark against the sky. It was easy to see that this was a place of execution. The soldiers tore off Jesus's clothes and nailed his outstretched arms to the beam. Then they lifted him with the beam on to a post and nailed his feet to it. Alongside Jesus they crucified two criminals, one to the right and one to the left.

The Sun beat down and sweat poured into the eyes of the condemned men. In order to breathe, they had to put their weight on their nailed feet. Above each cross, the soldiers fixed a sign with the name and crime of each condemned man. Above Jesus's head, passers by could read the inscription: Jesus of Nazareth, King of the Jews.

A small group of priests gathered

The Death of Jesus

around Jesus's cross. 'Come down from the cross, King,' they cried. 'If you can, perhaps we will believe that you are the Son of God.'

The man being crucified on Jesus's left grimaced and said, 'You have helped others, Messiah. Now help us and help yourself.'

The other criminal rebuked his comrade, 'Do you not fear God even now, just before your death? We both deserve our punishment, but he has done nothing wrong.' Then he added, 'Jesus, remember me when you enter your kingdom.'

Jesus looked up at the condemned man. 'Do not be afraid,' he told the man, 'you will enter the kingdom with me this very day.'

The Sun was now high over Jerusalem. Somewhere within the walls of the city Jesus's disciples were hiding. They had not dared to accompany their Master to his execution in case they themselves had fallen into the hands of the Grand Council

and had been sentenced to death too. Only John stood beneath the cross. With him was Jesus's mother, Mary. She had also come to Jerusalem for the celebrations and during the night she had been told by the disciples what had happened. Now she wanted to stay on the execution ground till the very end. Jesus looked down at her from the cross. 'Mother, now he will be your son,' he said, meaning John. To John he said, 'Please, look after her.'

While the soldiers drew lots beneath the cross as to who would have Jesus's clothes, the priests were preparing a lamb to sacrifice in the temple in Jerusalem. Jesus was dying. At about three in the afternoon his head dropped. 'It is over,' he said and died.

The soldiers wanted to be sure that the condemned man was really dead. One of

them took a spear and drove it into Jesus's side and from the wound flowed blood and water.

During the afternoon, two men came to the execution ground. They brought with them funeral linen and perfumed ointments. John knew both of them. One was called Joseph and came from Arimathea. The other was a Pharisee called Nicodemus. Both were disciples of Jesus, but did not say so publicly because they were afraid of the priests. The men took Jesus's body down from the cross, anointed it and wrapped it in linen. Then they placed it in a grave hollowed out of the rock in Joseph's garden. Before the first star came out, signalling the start of the Easter festivities, they had rolled a large rock across the entrance to the cave.

Night fell over Jerusalem. It concealed sickness, fear, the misery of the disciples, betrayal and a dead body which lay in a gorge beneath the city walls. The dead man in the gorge was Judas. In the morning, when he had heard about the death sentence passed on Jesus, he had felt remorse and had run to see the high priests. 'I have betrayed an innocent man,' he cried, but they turned away from him. 'What is that to us?' they said. 'That is your affair.' Judas threw the thirty pieces of silver into the temple and, unconsolable, ran along the city walls. When he saw a solitary tree, he hanged himself in his despair, but the branch could not withstand the weight of his body and it snapped. Judas plunged into the gorge, and died even before Jesus, whom he had betrayed.

The Death of Jesus

Jesus Lives

It was Sunday, the first day after the great festival and the third day since Jesus's death. In the late afternoon two men walked along the road from Jerusalem. They were downcast and sad.

'I cannot believe that the women who went to the grave this morning saw angels there,' sighed one.

'The angels are supposed to have told them that he was not there. They say he is alive,' said the other. 'Peter and John also went up there. The rock had been rolled away from the grave and there was nothing inside except the funeral linen.'

The men came to the little village of Emmaus. The shadows were already lengthening when an unknown pilgrim approached them. 'What are you talking about?' he asked them.

'The men stopped. 'You must be the only man in Jerusalem who does not know what happened these last few days,' said one of the men, whose name was Cleopas.

'And what happened?' asked the pilgrim.

'Our Grand Council sentenced Jesus of Nazareth to death. It is three days since he died on the cross, and we had hoped that he was the promised Messiah.'

'But why are you so sad?' asked the pilgrim. 'Did not Jesus say to you that on the third day he would rise from the dead?'

'Yes, he did say that,' sighed Cleopas. 'But it is so difficult to believe it.'

'You simply do not understand,' said the pilgrim. 'The Messiah had to die because he had taken man's fate and man's sins on to himself. These brought him to the cross, but death has no power over the Son of God.'

Cleopas thought for a moment. 'Some

people believed that our Messiah would deliver us from the power of the Romans,' he said.

'He delivered you from the power of evil, which is in all men,' replied the pilgrim. 'His death opened the door to Heaven for you.'

Soon afterwards, the men reached Emmaus and the unknown pilgrim began to take his leave of them. 'Stay with us,' they urged him. 'It is already evening. Where would you go at this time of night?'

All three went into a house. When they had sat down to supper, the pilgrim gave thanks to God, took the bread and began to break it. Then Cleopas and his companion realized that the pilgrim was Jesus, and at that very moment he vanished.

The men jumped up from the table. 'Why did we not realize before?' they asked each other in amazement. 'Did our hearts not burn with joy when he spoke to us on the road?' They left their supper and hurried back to Jerusalem. 'We must tell Peter and the others about all this,' they said.

They reached the city during the night. They knocked at the door of the house where the disciples were hiding. The disciples were still afraid of the Grand Council and had fastened their door securely so that no stranger could enter, but they knew Cleopas and his companion well.

'Cleopas,' cried the disciples one after the other, as soon as the visitors entered, 'Jesus has truly risen from the grave and has appeared to Peter.'

Peter stood in the middle of the group, his eyes shining with joy. Jesus was alive and was not angry that Peter had denied him in Caiaphas's courtyard.

Cleopas began to recount how they too had seen the Master, but before they had finished Jesus was there among them. Some of the disciples were frightened. They thought it was a ghost.

Then Jesus said, 'It is really me. I am of flesh and blood.' Then he asked them to give him something to eat.

The disciples gave Jesus a piece of baked fish. They could not take their eyes off their Master. It really was him!

They all looked forward to telling Thomas, who was not with them at night, about the resurrection of Jesus, but Thomas frowned and said, 'I do not believe you, and I will not believe you until I see him with my own eyes and touch the wounds made by the nails and the soldiers' spears.'

A week later Jesus came among the disciples again. This time Thomas was there too. 'Thomas, look at me,' said Jesus and showed him his injured wrists and the wound in the side. 'Touch me and do not doubt any longer that I am alive.'

Thomas stopped frowning at once. 'You are my Lord, my God,' he cried joyfully.

For forty days the resurrected Jesus continued to meet people. On one occasion there were more than five hundred, but usually he came to see the disciples. 'Go to your people and find friends for me,' he told them. 'Christen them in the name of the Father and the Son and the Holy Ghost and teach them everything I have taught you. Do not fear. I am the great king. I have all the power in Heaven and on Earth and I will stay with people until the end of time.'

On the fortieth day Jesus said goodbye to his disciples. 'Do not leave Jerusalem until God's Holy Spirit comes to you,' he told them. 'He will give you strength and you will bear my witness throughout the world.'

Finally, they all went off together to Bethany. Jesus blessed them for the last time and then a cloud enveloped him. Who knows how long they would have stood there and looked up into the sky, if they had not heard a voice. 'Why are you standing there looking up into the sky?' it said. 'Jesus has left you and returned to his Father, but he will come to you once again.'

The disciples turned around and saw two angels dressed in dazzling white robes. They remembered what Jesus had told them and returned to Jerusalem. A new life awaited them. What would it bring them? What would happen when they spread the word of the Son of God throughout the world? Then, together with some women among whom was Mary, Jesus's mother, they prayed and waited until the Spirit of God gave them wisdom and strength.

Jesus Lives

The Apostle Peter

Ten days had passed since Jesus returned to his heavenly Father, and his relatives, friends and disciples were still together. A man called Matthew took the place of Judas, and a circle of twelve apostles emerged. On the morning of the tenth day, they all praised God, but suddenly they fell silent. A violent wind seemed to blow through the house. Such was the noise that a roaring filled the whole house and tongues of fire settled on each of them.

The strange noise attracted a crowd of onlookers to the house. 'What is going on?' they asked in amazement. Jesus's disciples rushed out of the house into the street, raising their hands to the sky and glorifying God.

'But that is impossible,' the people said in wonder. 'They are speaking Latin, Greek, Arabic, the language of Medes and Babylonians, and they are just uneducated village men.'

Then Peter addressed the crowd and said, 'Are you surprised at what you hear? The Spirit of God entered us in the form of fiery tongues and taught us how to speak. The Spirit of God was sent to us by Jesus, the man you allowed to be crucified.'

The men from Jerusalem were greatly disturbed by what they had seen and heard. 'What are we supposed to do?' they asked. 'We did not want Jesus to die.'

'Jesus is not dead,' said Peter. 'He has risen from his grave and now he is with his Father in Heaven. If you want to understand what has happened, believe in him.'

A few days later Peter and John went to the temple. At the gate sat a number of beggars, and among them a paralysed man. The paralysed man held out his hand to Peter.

Peter said to him, 'I have neither gold nor silver, but everything I have I shall give you. In the name of Jesus, stand up and walk.'

The paralysed man stood up and his legs supported him. He began to jump around and he was so overcome with joy that a crowd of people soon noticed him.

Peter was still speaking when the temple guard appeared in the courtyard near the pillars of Solomon. 'You are not allowed to teach people about that blasphemer, Jesus of Nazareth!' they shouted at Peter and John. They arrested them and took them off to the prison for the night.

The next day Peter and John were

brought before Annas, Caiaphas and the other priests and scribes. 'What happened to that paralysed man? Who healed him?' they asked.

Peter stood up straight. For a long time now, he had had no fear of the high priests. The Spirit of God had filled him with courage, wisdom and strength. He did not even fear death. He knew after death he would meet his Master again. 'I will answer you gladly,' he said. 'It was Jesus of Nazareth who restored that man's health and strength. His power healed him.'

The high priests frowned. They ordered Peter and John to be taken away and then they began to confer. 'God has performed a true miracle via these men, and some people in Jerusalem know about it. We must release them, but we must strictly forbid them from ever talking to people about Jesus of Nazareth again.'

Peter and John returned happily to their

Jesus had risen from the dead. The people of Jerusalem listened to them and continued to bring the sick to them. They even brought them out into the street when Peter was passing, so, at the very least, his shadow would fall on them.

The high priests did not attempt to heal anyone, because they were filled with hatred. Once again they ordered the arrest of the apostles, but in the middle of the night a messenger from God opened the prison gates. 'Go to the temple and continue to teach the people,' the messenger told them and led them out into the street.

The guards were sent to arrest the apostles immediately, and when they were brought in, the high priest began by saying, 'We forbade you to teach people about that man, but you did not obey us and you have filled the whole of Jerusalem with his teaching.'

Peter answered at once. 'We should

friends. There were already several thousand of them. They prayed together and broke bread in each other's houses, as Jesus had taught them. No one was needy, because they all shared everything they had.

The apostles did not obey the high priests. They went on telling people how

obey God and not people. That is why we did not obey your orders. Now before the whole Grand Council we bear witness that Jesus, the man you denounced, is the Lord and the Messiah.'

This answer enraged the high priests. Then a wise Pharisee rose to his feet, a man named Gamaliel, and said, 'Think well about what you do to these men. If their work and teaching comes from men, then it will come to nothing; but if it comes from God, you should not attempt to destroy these followers of Jesus.'

Finally the Council heeded Gamaliel's words and the apostles were released.

However, the high priests of Jerusalem did not follow the advice of the wise Pharisee Gamaliel for long. One of the Jesus's followers, a man called Stephen, was banished from Jerusalem and there outside the city he was stoned to death.

A young Pharisee called Saul of Tarsus had seen the stoning. He approved of Stephen's death. He hated people who followed Jesus of Nazareth and decided he would destroy the new teaching at its very roots. After Stephen's death, he went from house to house, accompanied by the temple guard, and arrested people and threw them into prison.

This brutal campaign drove Jesus's friends from the city. They scattered to all four corners of the country. Some reached Phoenicia, others the island of Cyprus, others still the Syrian town of Antioch. Everywhere they went they told people about the Son of God.

The apostle Peter stayed in Jerusalem, but after a time he decided to go and see Jesus's friends, scattered as they were all over the Roman Empire. He visited many places, before he was invited to the coastal town of Joppa.

'Come quickly,' they told him. 'A sister of ours called Dorcas had died. She was a kind woman who helped everyone, and we do not want to lose her.'

Peter set off immediately, and with the power of Jesus he brought Dorcas back to life.

God even sent Peter into the house of a Roman centurion called Cornelius. Peter baptized Cornelius and his whole family, and when he returned to Jerusalem, he said, 'God told me that all men that aspire to His kingdom may enter it. Not just people from the chosen nation, but gentiles too.'

In Jerusalem Peter was thrown into prison again and once more he was released. A long life and many journeys lay before him. He healed the sick, comforted the grieving and taught everyone about the Son of God and his kingdom. His Master had once given him the name Peter, and he did, indeed, become the rock upon which Jesus has built his church for two thousand years.

The Apostle Paul

The Apostle Paul

The young Pharisee Saul of Tarsus continued to pursue the followers of the new teaching that was spreading through Jerusalem. The fact that Jesus's friends had fled from him did not help. He even wanted to pursue them to the places where they had found a new home. The Grand Council supported this campaign of violence. He was given guides and taken to the city of Damascus in Syria.

After several days' travel, Saul finally saw the walls of Damascus. He checked to make sure that the journey had not damaged the letter of the high priest, given him as a message of goodwill to the scribes of Damascus and prepared to enter the city. Suddenly he was surrounded by an enormous light. It was brighter than the Sun and a human figure emerged from its centre. Saul fell to the earth in terror.

'Saul, why are you persecuting me!' said the stranger.

Saul raised his head. 'Who are you, Lord?'

'I am Jesus,' replied the man. 'The Jesus you are persecuting.'

'Lord, what do you want me to do?' asked Saul fearfully.

'I am sending you to the Gentiles, to bring them to God,' said Jesus. 'But go now to Jerusalem.'

After a short time, Saul got up from the ground and rubbed his eyes, but he could not see anything. The brilliant light had blinded him. The guides had to take him by the arm and lead him into the city. They found him a bed in the house of a man called Judas. Saul stayed there three days. In those three days he did not eat nor drink, but simply thought about what he had experienced.

At that time there lived in Damascus a devout man named Ananias. Jesus said to Ananias, 'Go to the house of Judas and ask for Saul of Tarsus. When they bring him to you, put your hand upon him so he may see again.'

Ananias was afraid. 'But that is the man who is persecuting your friends in Jerusalem. He has them whipped and thrown into prison. He has come here to destroy us.'

'Do not be afraid,' said Jesus. 'Saul will no longer harm any of my friends. I have chosen him to spread my teachings to the people of many nations.'

Ananias hesitated no longer, and did what Jesus had asked him.

Saul of Tarsus could see again. He stayed with the Damascus disciples and they could see how their enemy had changed.

Saul had barely recovered from his long fast, when he began to preach in the Jewish synagogues that Jesus was the Messiah and the Son of God. At first the scribes could not believe their ears. Then they exploded in anger. 'We will kill him,' they resolved, 'and we shall watch the gates of Damascus day and night so he does not escape from us.'

Saul heard of the plot the scribes had hatched against him and wondered how to escape from this danger. Finally, in the middle of the night, his friends lowered him from the city walls on a rope.

After three years Saul returned to Jerusalem. He sought out Peter and told him everything that had happened. The disciples no longer feared him. They no longer felt threatened by him, and when he himself was threatened by danger, they helped him to get to his native city, Tarsus.

In far off regions, in the cities where Jesus's friends had taken refuge after Stephen's death, there were now many people who believed in the Messiah, in Christ. In the Syrian city of Antioch, they began to call themselves followers of Christ, or Christians. Among them were many gentiles, both men and women, who had previously worshipped all kinds of gods and idols and who had never heard of the one and only God. Saul too went to join the Christians of Antioch. He stayed with them for a whole year, and then set off on further journeys.

In many cities of the huge Roman Empire, Saul told the Christians, 'Gird yourselves with truth, put on the armour of righteousness and the sandals of peace. Overcome evil with good, and never forget that without merciful love you are absolutely nothing. Love is patient, kind. Love knows no envy. Love is not conceited nor boastful. It does not act dishonourably, nor does it seek benefit nor apportion blame. Whatever happens, love endures.'

Soon he became more widely known by the name of Paul. He had many adventures on his journeys. He often only narrowly escaped death, but no dangers or threats could turn him away from Jesus, whom he had seen that day before the gates of Damascus.

MEDITERRANEAN SEA

Capernaum
Cana
Magdala
Nazareth
Bethsaida
GALILEE
LAKE

Samaria

Jordan River

Arimathea

Emmaus
Jerusalem
Jericho
Bethany
Bethlehem
DEAD
SEA
Hebron